If you are ready to make changes i[n] [...] for you. Through a series of person[al] [...] applications, the authors pause regularly to ask readers to explore the issues in their own lives. It is more participatory than a how-to book and definitely more compelling and enjoyable!

—Stephanie Johanns
Customer Services Director,
Aliant Communications
Nebraska's First Lady

Sage advice provided through personal vignettes laced with humor — a must for all who want to improve their quality of life. Jo and Wes pick up lessons in life where Chicken Soup for the Soul *left off.*

—Diane Allensworth, Ph.D.
Professor Emeritus
Kent State University

Throughout history, people have found a way to excel in spite of obstacles and set-backs, and that excellence comes to those who are able to take any situation and glean from it the most helpful elements. The authors demonstrate how the "test of fire" creates the strongest and purest steel as they gently nudge readers into a greater appreciation of their own gifts. These stories need be read by everyone, shared with those we love, and then put into the practice of creating healthier, happier people.

—Jim Kern, Ph.D.
Education Consultant, Speaker
and Author of *Build The Fort Today*

Excellent…this is a heart healthy book. Dr. Owens-Nauslar and Dr. Sime take the hard and "real" stuff in life and present it in such a way that it motivates you to embrace your fears, and inspires you to create your own masterpiece…YOU!

—Rhonda Revelle
Husker Softball, Head Coach
University of Nebraska-Lincoln

Making **DO**
out of
Doo-Doo

Lessons in Life
for Hardiness,
Health & Fitness

JoAnne Owens-Nauslar, LBWA/EdD
&
Wes Sime, PhD[2]

ISBN 1-886225-44-3

Cover design by Angie Johnson Art Productions

Dageforde Publishing, Inc.
122 South 29th Street
Lincoln, Nebraska 68510
Phone: (402) 475-1123   FAX: (402) 475-1176

Visit our Website at
http://www.dageforde.com
email: info@dageforde.com

Printed in the United States of America

10   9   8   7   6   5   4   3   2   1

Dedication

The inspiration for this book comes from the people we have encountered throughout life. You may be one of many who has had a part in shaping our lives and tickling our humor button. Each step along the way has been forged with the emotions we have felt as a part of meeting the challenges in life, thus, *Making Do out of Doo-Doo.*

For each of us, the most gratitude and appreciation for the patience and tolerance of our time, commitment, and dedication in writing this book goes to our spouses. Maxine, who has always been there amidst the trials and tribulations for Wes, and is a source of inspiration with her common sense, wisdom, and strong character. Red, whose zest for living and incredible sense of humor puts the wind beneath Jo's wings.

To the teachers and family members who have taught us "lots," we say thanks.

Table of Contents

Acknowledgments

We wish to thank the reviewers of our early manuscript—Mary Ann Mellor for her suggestions, editing, and kind remarks that spurred us to complete this book. Kari Beckenhauer was very helpful with her critique and suggestions. We want to acknowledge our publisher, Linda Dageforde of Dageforde Publishing. Her guidance and awesome sense of humor made the revisions and completion of this work a pleasant and educational experience.

Introduction

Life is a series of peaks and valleys with a lot of plateaus in between. Sometimes, the challenging events in our lives do not seem fair. How can some people have so much and others so little? Why is it some individuals have to search long and hard to find opportunity and others have it "fall in their laps?" Why do some people always seem to be having fun while others appear so unhappy? Why do some continue to bounce back while others seem destined to be stuck?

This book contains stories about a variety of serious and/or funny events in our lives that were unplanned and less than ideal, but had a very significant impact on how we lead our lives today. As a result of these events, we were forced to make accommodations, adjustments, and advancements that ultimately improved our lives, thus *Making Do out of Doo-Doo*. In so doing, we became wiser, calmer, more sensitive, better listeners, better teachers, more philanthropic, and more understanding family members. Writing this book helped us articulate the lessons in life that we have learned about dealing with stress, maintaining relationships, staying healthy and fit, practicing laughter, and feeling good about sharing our souls.

Along the way, we have sometimes asked "Why me?" but we soon learned that, the better question was "Why not me?" Perhaps there is an important lesson in life that is supposed to be learned from every bump in the road. Very likely, we appreciate the smooth parts of our journey through life specifically because of those "bumps" in our past experience, not in spite of them. While we may be very content with the smooth, flat, satisfying parts of our life, some of the most important growth lessons have occurred because of the trials of life. We have been embarrassed, sad, happy, obnoxious, messed up, confused, hurt, frightened, and as a result, we have become bold in our beliefs. We intend to hit you in the head, the heart, and the gut. We are sharing our stories in hopes that some good and healther choices will come from our experiences in *Making Do out of Doo-Doo*. We are not concerned if you do not like all our stories. We think it even better if we provoke you a bit. However, we don't want you to "get your colon in a wad" over our forthright and folksy presentation style. Nevertheless, we do admonish you to "Get with it." Take the challenge that we put forth to get into action and strive to be better.

Even though vital statistics might show that Americans are living longer than we did 50 to 100 years ago, it is not necessarily because we are healthier as individuals. Rather, it is modern science, medicine, and technology that are the major contributing factors to longevity in this century. As individuals, we could do so much more to live better and longer. Come on, America, get off the slow wagon and get on the "band wagon for the health of it."

As you read our stories about the real issues in life—family, faith, health, fitness, money, and relationships—we encourage you to focus on the balance in your life. Are you devoting the necessary time to the vital issues that contribute to your health and happiness? Perhaps these messages will prompt you to make the changes that are right for you.

Part I of the book begins with stories about the challenges in life that we have labeled the *Doo-Doo*. Each story is concluded with several lessons in life that could be learned from the experience. Finally, each story also has a list of action solutions for you that add up to *Making Do*.

Part II of the book includes sections featuring several topics summarizing the essentials of making and maintaining the lifestyle changes for health, hardiness, and fitness. These are things we feel need to be done if one is serious about living long and living well in a high performance body.

Our intent is to stir a range of emotions and stimulate you to become more motivated about a healthier lifestyle, both physically and emotionally. To accomplish that goal, sometimes we opt to make you laugh but sometimes it is more important that you feel a little uncomfortable about your habits in life. Perhaps a gentle nudge is needed to make you take responsibility. From all of life's events (being fired, losing a friend or family member, illness, impairment, or simply disappointment), we want you to find your spirit for living and your sense of emotional hardiness. Bounce back, be better, and *Make Do out of Doo-Doo*.

Remember, stories passed down through the generations can provide powerful insight and learning to kids about how to bounce back.

Part I

Establish a Spirit of Living and Hardiness

I have often pondered how my mom has coped with *Doo-Doo* in life. She has endured much and bounced back from many losses and traumatic situations. Both of her parents and her two brothers died prematurely. She quit high school because she was pregnant with me at age fifteen. She and my father married, but divorced after two years. She remarried shortly thereafter and then, later, had to deal with my stepdad's terminal illness and ultimate death. She was frequently alone and, at times, very lonely and depressed amidst the severe Wyoming winters. Underlying all of this tragedy, she also has struggled with a weight issue and a bit of family dysfunction.

Despite being a high school dropout, a mother at age sixteen, a divorcee at age eighteen, and a single parent of two young babies alone, I am proud to say that my mom has completed her GED and two college certifications. In addition, she was married to my stepfather for forty-five years and has kept the family together during that time and beyond by working steadily to support herself without outside assistance. My emotions come to the surface very easily when I think about all she has endured and accomplished. These are tears of joy, pride, and occasionally of sadness, but, most importantly, they are healthy tears.

Like my mom, it seems that sometimes people are able to cope very well with seemingly overwhelming stressors in life simply because they have absolutely no other choice. When your only choice is to deal with it or give up, most people find a way to get on with their lives. However, some of us have the capability of dealing with life's stressors better than others. I believe my mother's ability to cope and bounce back exists because she developed a "spirit for living."

Mom always seems to *Make Do out of Doo-Doo*. Her zest for living, combined with her ability to overcome trauma and loss, have been a valuable legacy and lesson for me throughout my life. For my mom, her passion is to give to others and be devoted to loving her family. It has been tough on her, no doubt, but she has been a pillar of strength and a model for good coping skills. Here are some of Mom's coping skills commonly used in the midst of a crisis.

Mom's Great Coping Skills:

- A good cry. She calls this a boo-hoo session.
- A good laugh follows the good cry and then she usually cries again.
- Then a walking-talking session with a good friend or relative to mull over stuff while getting in touch with nature and the elements. During that session, she always counts all the things for which she is blessed and thankful. These include her family, house, faith, job, community, "bubba" (the human cat), and friends, just to name a few.
- She then has her favorite beverage…a good cup of coffee. I know it's caffeine, but give her a break. She doesn't drink alcohol, she walks on the treadmill every morning, she picks up garbage others throw out on the roadside, she recycles, and she has stopped smoking. What the heck; a little caffeine shouldn't hurt!
- She concludes the whole process with a reassuring statement: "I feel better now."

Keep in mind, Mom's great coping cycle may be repeated numerous times before a situation is under control, but the pattern is usually the same and she is a model for all who know her. I have the greatest respect for Mom, what her life has been like, and what she has been able to accomplish.

Reach deep down inside and find your spirit for living. What is your driving reason to go on and keep striving to overcome? Be mindful, there may be more than one very good reason.

Lessons in Life

- Sometimes life is not fair. Trauma and loss (*Doo-Doo*) are part of life.
- Developing a spirit (reason) for living is a first step if you are to bounce back from any challenge in life.
- Coping strategies are learned behaviors. Expect to be challenged as a process of learning.
- It is important to have strong role models and people who provide support as you cope with difficult issues in life.

Action Solutions

- Review your life history to discover the experiences that give you the drive and determination to strive to overcome.

- Who is(are) your role model(s) for great coping skills?

- What can you do right now to capitalize on strengths of your past?

- Itemize your coping skills and how they came to be.

The Purple Sweater

My biological parents were divorced before my third birthday. There are very few clues about their breakup because neither of them will discuss much about their relationship. I'm convinced that the reasons for their divorce included being teenage parents having two toddlers as well as occasional unemployment, family meddling, and general incompatibility.

My contacts with my biological father were limited during my elementary school years. As I grew into my middle school years, it became more important to me to know more about and spend time with my biological dad. My mom had remarried two days before my third birthday, but I still wanted to know my father. I knew I had my father's facial features as evidenced by the few pictures of my dad, but what I did not know was whether I had his love, concern, or respect. In fact, I was not certain that he even cared about my well-being.

The few childhood memories I have of him are riding his roping horse named Old New (think about that for a minute and you may put the book down) and driving through the pasture to see the buffalo he raised. Throughout the years, I had sent many birthday and Father's Day cards and invited him to several graduations and my wedding, but I had never received a response from him. It had hurt me a great deal to have never had the pleasure of his presence at any major event in my life.

One can spend hours in tears (and I have) trying to better understand why a parent was not responsive. I had two unanswered questions: 1) Why were my natural parents divorced (was it because of an unintended child — me)? and 2) Why did my biological father choose not to be a part of my growing up?

When the people with the answers do not provide information, it is natural to make up our own. For me the answers were: Maybe my parents truly were incompatible; maybe the divorce was so traumatic and ugly that my biological dad just wanted out with no strings attached; maybe as teenagers, my parents knew little about child rearing and relationships; or, maybe my biological father had another relationship already forming. The list of potential explanations went on and on. Therefore, I concluded— erroneously—that each of my explanations were true at one time or another, because I did not have access to the truth through my parents' experience.

For many years I grieved my relationship with my father, however there comes a point where one must consider when to let go; "If your horse is dead...dismount!" That is, I had to stop fretting about the excess baggage from my parents' divorce—it wasn't mine to bear. (The importance of letting go of things you can't control is discussed in greater detail in the chapter titled "If Your Horse Is Dead...Dismount!") I still had to deal with both my fond memories and the leftover hurts manifested by a childhood gift that remind me of my absentee father. The only gift I remember receiving from my father was a purple sweater. It arrived at Christmastime when I was fourteen years old. My twelve-year-old brother Dick did not receive a gift from our father that Christmas, so my purple sweater took on a very bittersweet meaning.

I had always shared everything with Dick, but this gift did not seem to be share-friendly; rather, it became symbolic of the guilt I felt. Because Dick didn't get a gift, was I the favored child? Did Dad not love Dick? Did he just forget to take Dick's gift out of his pickup? Or did we overlook Dick's present from Dad somewhere under the tree? When I finally realized that there was no gift for my little brother, I hurt for him. After that, I recall, we did not have opportunities to spend as much time with my father. The events that unfolded that Christmas Day brought me to the stark realization that I needed to stop struggling with relationship issues that I probably would never get resolved.

I never wore that frilly button-down purple sweater, but it is still in my cedar chest some thirty-six years later. I take it out once a year on my birthday and it always stirs lots of emotion. I have often wondered how my life would have been different — not better or worse, just different — if my father had been a part of my growing up years. The struggle about the feelings we have for our parents takes us down lots of emotional paths including joy, happiness, sadness, anger, and guilt. In my case, coupled with those feelings were many unanswered questions.

As I have passed the half-century mark of life, I am saddened by the fact that my biological father who still lives close to my other family members (on my mom's side) has remained a virtual stranger to me and to my brother. Despite our efforts to connect with Dad, Dick is particularly distressed by the fact that two of his three children, ages thirteen and twenty-one, have never met their grandfather. For my part, I am still bothered by the fact that my father and I know very little about each other.

I have had only one opportunity to express my bewilderment and disappointment about my childhood to my dad. Shortly after my wedding in 1981, my husband and I went to Custer, South Dakota, specifically to find my father, and we did. Driving down the main street on our way to his home, I recognized him in his pickup going the other direction. I shouted to my husband, "Red, there's my father!" As we turned around and drove back to catch up to him, I questioned whether I was ready for this encounter. But instinctively, I shouted out the window to him, "Dad, we'll buy you coffee."

During coffee and great conversation (mostly between my father and Red), I became determined to find a private moment to speak candidly with my father about our relationship. While they talked about cows, politics, and the weather, I was able to muster the courage to plan a confrontation with my father as we walked to his car.

Alone with him for a few moments (as Red wandered off), I felt compelled to share my thirty years of frustration over his neglect as an absentee father. At first, no words of frustration came out, so I started to say goodbye thinking I needed to get out of there. Then suddenly, I felt an overwhelming compulsion to grab him for a hug and kiss him goodbye. I found myself imbedded in his big barreled chest crying as hard as I have ever cried.

Amidst all the tears, I blurted out, "Dad, I still have the purple sweater you gave me and I don't understand why it's so hard to get to know you. You need to know that Dick and I want nothing material from you. However, we do want you to know us, respect us, and acknowledge our accomplishments. You have three wonderful grandchildren who ask about you and we don't have very many answers for them. My brother and I have the skills to make what money we need, so don't be worried about us asking for money or inheritance. I love you, Dad, and I think you're a neat dude, but how would I even know that for sure from my limited personal experience with you?"

He did not respond to my outburst of emotion. We turned and walked to our separate vehicles, both of us fighting back tears. I'm not sure much has changed from that encounter, but at least I said my piece. I tried not to be disrespectful, but I definitely felt better because I had told him some of what I felt.

My Dad and I have had a few conversations since then; they are usually short and are not as emotional as the meeting after coffee. Ironically, my father's grandson, Heath (who he has never met), is now attending college ninety miles away from where my father lives. Sometime in the next year, I intend to visit my nephew and take him to meet his grandfather. I know that this experience will serve to satisfy much of my brother's frustration, and it will allow Heath to ask his questions of his grandfather directly. It is sad for me to think that Dick probably won't be able to participate in that monumental family meeting.

I have decided that I intend to live to be at least ninety-six years young and when I die, I expect to still have the purple sweater.

Lessons in Life

- If parents don't tell kids the truth about a traumatic experience in their lives, the kids will likely come to their own conclusions, often blaming themselves inappropriately.
- You have many childhood experiences (both good and bad) that influence how you interact with people today.
- You may regret not taking the time to be there when someone needs you.

- Consider whether there are interpersonal conflicts in your life that might influence your future in some positive or negative way.
- Always mend your fences or rethink your behaviors in the midst of conflict or confusion as soon as the opportunity arises.

Action Solutions

- Describe a situation where you may have caused someone to be distressed by not attending to their needs.

_____

_____

_____

- Provide insight into how you can lessen the stress for someone by offering some communication.

_____

_____

_____

- List some actions that you might need to take in order to put some difficult issues to rest.

_____

_____

_____

Getting Bitten and Burned

Past experiences color our perspective in future stressful situations. A couple of childhood experiences help to clarify this point. At the age of nine or ten, I was visiting my cousin at his family's farm and was bitten by a large watch dog who mistook me for an intruder. It happened in a dark area where I did not see the dog coming. I was stunned by the unexpected attack as much as I was bothered by the pain of the dog bite.

It was especially scary at the time because there was some concern that the dog might have had rabies. Though my wounds healed easily and the dog was not found to be rabid (which spared me painful treatment procedures), I still am sensitized by that incident. As an adult forty-five years later, if I am surprised by a strange dog barking or growling, I freeze in my tracks with a chill running down my back (even if the dog is chained or behind a fence). This is a natural fight or flight reaction that becomes exaggerated.

Ironically, the fight or flight stress response is what animals can sense in humans who are afraid. As a result, animals will often take advantage by continuing their intimidating actions. There is no doubt that my stress reactions to dogs are directly related to that childhood incident. It clearly compromises my stress coping ability to some small or large extent depending on how well prepared I am to deal with a stressful situation.

A couple of years later (at age twelve), I had another stressful experience (this one was emotional) that remains imbedded in my brain. The family had a big reunion on a hot summer day.

Someone brought a big chunk of dry ice for the punch bowl to surprise everyone. My cousins and I were all excited to be there, having heard about (but never seen) the steam emitted when the dry ice hit the liquid. My uncle was breaking up the block of ice into smaller pieces when a small chunk fell on the floor. Being a prankster at that age, I picked it up and quickly dropped it down the back of my cousin's sun dress. What I didn't know, of course, was that dry ice will burn if it stays in contact with the skin for more than one to two seconds. Fortunately, my uncle saw what happened and quickly shook my cousin's clothing until the piece of dry ice fell to the floor. What he did next, was quite devastating for me.

I am sure that my uncle wanted to impress upon me and the other cousins how dangerous it was to play with dry ice and perhaps curb the prankish behavior. In so doing, he singled me out and chastised me severely for what I had done. He made a big scene about the fact that my cousin could have incurred a severe burn if the dry ice stayed in contact with her skin for more than a couple of seconds. The rest of the family joined in to make the effect even more dramatic. For the rest of that family gathering, I was shunned by nearly everyone, including my cousins.

Only in recent years have I come to understand what the word "shunning" means in some religious orders and what the effect of being ostracized can be on a young person's psyche. To this day, when I return to Minnesota for family gatherings, occasionally I encounter a couple of relatives involved in the dry ice incident. I have to fight back the sensation to cringe on the inside as if I am reliving that experience of shame and shunning that occurred so many years before.

Lessons in Life

- Be aware of the potential impact of severe punishment on kids, especially those who might be sensitive to particular kinds of embarrassment.

- Be aware of adult experiences that may be tainted by the impact of childhood traumas. For example, interpersonal communication among shy individuals may be due to social discomfort incurred during childhood.

- Be aware of physically traumatic experiences that may cause delayed stress reactions. These might occur as a result of a car accident, cuts, sport injuries, or sexually inappropriate touching.

Action Solutions

- Describe an emotional situation that occurred in your childhood that may still have some impact on how you function as an adult in work and personal relationships.

_____

_____

_____

- Describe a physically traumatizing situation that may have occurred in childhood or young adulthood that affects you now.

_____

_____

_____

- Lay out a plan as to how you might overcome moderately traumatic experiences so they do not have lasting effects.

_____

_____

_____

Doing Chores Does Not Constitute Child Abuse

JoAnne's Chores: One of my tasks, growing up, was to feed the horses and gather the eggs at night—not too much to handle for a ten year old. On a cold December evening, however, I "blew off" doing my chores with the rationalization of "Who would know?" I didn't think horses and chickens could complain in a language my parents could understand, so I skipped out on this occasion. Much to my surprise, the hungry horses started nickering about 3:00 A.M. and that was unusual. That woke my dad, who went outside to see what the fuss was about. The horses were hungry and a skunk was in the hen house eating the eggs I had not gathered.

The consequence of my negligence was powerful. The eggs the skunk ate were part of the family breakfast for the next morning, so Mom and Dad taught me a *lesson in life*. I had only dry toast for breakfast, while everyone else had a full breakfast complete with eggs. My meager dry toast breakfast served as a reminder of the importance of doing my chores.

Wes' Chores: When I was about eight years old, one of my chores was to go the pasture each evening and chase the cow up to the barn to be milked. When I got her into the barnyard, I was supposed to put the electric wire across the fence lane to keep her from going back out to the pasture.

My dad had instructed me to carefully grab and hold onto the wooden handle attached to the end of the electric wire when I opened or closed that fence. He warned me, "You be careful to handle only the wood insulator around the wire so you don't get a shock." On the first day I went out alone to do my chores, I must have gotten careless in how I gripped the handle to pick up the electric wire because I got a shock that jolted my entire body (I think even my teeth rattled). It was a very scary experience; not life threatening, but nasty enough to keep the animals, as well as me, away from the wire.

When that shock hit me, I ran crying across the farm yard to where my dad was working. He was sorry that I had gotten a shock, but not very understanding about my refusal to go back to the fence. He said, "You should be able to pick up the wooden handle without getting a shock." He carefully explained to me again that the wood served as insulation against the electricity, therefore, I should not be afraid. However, nothing he said could ease my anxiety over the possibility of getting another jolt when I went back to close the electric fence behind the cow.

I wanted him to come and handle the electric wire problem for me, but he was not willing to do so. I recall that he was very patient, but persistent, in giving me very explicit instructions on how to hold the handle so as not to touch the wire. I was still afraid. Finally, he backed down and went along with me to show me, once again, the proper and safe way to hold the wooden handle. When it was finished, I recall his message was clear—"Tomorrow night you can do it yourself, and you must do it, Wes !"

Late the next afternoon, I left early to bring the cow in from the pasture. I was able to pick up the handle on the electric wire without incident, but then as I pulled hard to stretch to make the connection, I brushed my arm against the wire. WHAMO! When the jolt hit me, I must have been leaning back because the shock left me lying on the ground. Of course, I was not hurt, but I was really mad. I bounced up with vengeance and ran across the yard screaming outrages at my father.

When I reached him, he tried to calm me, but I was furious. The angrier I got, the more humorous it must have been because he laughed, which made me even more furious. This happened once or twice more before I figured out the trick of holding the insulator properly. Each time the shock got me, I became more and more furious at my father, blaming him, of course, for the fact that I kept brushing against the bare wire. He never got upset at me for my nasty attitude, but he did seem to enjoy the frustration involved in my "hard knock lessons in life." I'm sure it was very humorous to see me so angry at a little ol' piece of wood that could "bite back" if you didn't handle it right.

In retrospect, my father's patience and persistence were remarkable. He insisted that I face up to the task and keep returning to try again. He could have caved in and let me out of doing my chores. He could have disciplined me harshly for my behavior toward him. Instead, he made me face my fears. I eventually overcame my fear of electricity and became more hardy and confident because of the experience. I did learn that you gotta be careful around things that can "bite back" if you are careless.

Lessons in Life

- When *Doo-Doo* happens (and there was a lot of it around the barnyard), it does not pay to get angry at others.
- You must face up to your fears in order to overcome them; running away or avoidance is not the solution.
- Seek assistance when possible, but don't expect others to take over for you. It would not be in your best interest for others to solve your problem for you.
- Just do what you are supposed to do; there is a reason why the chores were assigned and need to be done.
- Remember the patience of your elders; someday you may be called upon to use it when your own children are disenchanted with their chores.

Action Solutions

- List a number of childhood chores that helped teach you about responsibility and the consequences of your actions or inaction.

- Recall situations in which you have been faced with very anxiety-provoking situations. How did you handle them? Who was there for you?

_____

_____

_____

- Lay out a strategy for handling your next difficult circumstance. How would you approach it differently based on past experience and insight?

_____

_____

_____

Everyone's Allowed an Occasional Failure

Mistakes and failures do happen, and everyone except the skydiver and life guard, are allowed an occasional miscue. These mistakes and failures, together with the consequences that follow, can be very powerful learning experiences. The critical factor is how we respond to having made a particular mistake.

When I was fourteen years old, I had a chance to take a Junior Life Saving class with students one year older than I. It was a big privilege to participate, and I really wanted to show that I could succeed among these older kids, who also happened to be all female. In the next to last session of the course, the instructor staged a mock rescue attempt to show us how dangerous it could be to try to rescue a drowning victim.

The instructor chose me to be the rescuer while he was mimicking the victim flailing his arms in the middle of the pool. I swam out to him, boldly and confidently following procedure. I got him into a proper rescue position (a cross-chest carry) with his back to me and my arms wrapped around his massive chest (he was 6'2", 200 lbs and I was 5'5", 135 lbs). As I began kicking vigorously to propel both of us slowly back to the edge of the pool, he went into a demonstration of what could happen to the rescuer trying to save a panic-stricken victim. He broke from my grip, spun around, grabbed me in a bear hug, and dragged me to the bottom of the ten-foot pool. I know that he took in a big breath of air, but I was so surprised by his actions that I didn't have the same opportunity.

What a desperate feeling it was to be suffocating and inhaling nothing but chlorine water. Eventually, he brought me back to the surface and hauled me back to the deck as I coughed and gasped for air. I am sure that it was an extremely meaningful demonstration for the class to have a real-life simulation of what could happen when attempting a rescue. Needless to say, this demonstration was more devastating than enlightening for me. I was "scared to death" by the suffocating experience. I felt humiliated and hurt, but most of all, I was angry that he had done this to me without prior warning. When I left the pool that day — I never returned!

All of my friends in the class got their Junior Life Saving Certificate, but I had quit. In spite of my parent's urgings and knowing that I had passed all the requirements for the class, I quit, I gave up, I didn't go back.

In retrospect, I think I refused to go back because I didn't know how to communicate my true feelings of anger and embarrassment to the instructor. I hated him for what he had done, but most of all, I hated the fact that I had let him defeat me. I spent the rest of that summer and the entire school year regretting the fact that I had quit. When I saw my friends and peers at school, I felt embarrassed and shamed by the experience thinking that everyone must know I had quit.

I had let my emotions overcome logic. I turned the anger on myself instead of confronting the instructor. Even though he was, in my view, wrong for what he had done to me in that pool, I suffered the feeling of failure.

Fortunately, the life saving class became available again the following summer with a different instructor and I enrolled. To my surprise, I was able to take Senior Life Saving without having the junior level certificate. I definitely needed to confront my fears and embarrassment from the previous summer in order to regain my self-esteem. Without that opportunity to bounce back, and *Make Do out of Doo-Doo*, I fear that I would have lost much of my confidence and initiative to take on any new challenge in the future.

As an adult, I have been able to overcome many professional and personal experiences that were challenging and sometimes devastating (like my drowning threat). By contrast, there have been other times when I needed the wisdom to let go and drop a project when it was clearly beyond hope. Regardless, I always know that I have given my best effort before bailing out on a project, in part, because of the humiliation from these past experiences. More importantly, I learned how bad it feels to have quit something you want to accomplish. That devastating experience and the nauseating feeling of "being a quitter" impacted me so much that I have never again had to say "I quit" when working toward goals that were important to me.

In retrospect, I wonder what would have happened if my parents had intervened to demand that I be given the certificate of completion or to protest the harshness of the rescuer demonstration. I think I learned more from the experience because they did not intervene. I had to deal with the consequences of my decision, for better or worse.

While writing this book, I decided to try to find my life saving instructor, forty years after taking his class. A few months ago, I drove 500 miles to the location where he worked and we talked about the life saving fiasco. Instead of holding a grudge, I was able to tell him how devastating that experience was (at the time), while sharing the fact that I learned a great deal about sticking with important goals. I found him to be a very likable guy with whom I shared many of the same life experiences. Ironically, he is in a position to be able to help me professionally and has offered to do so enthusiastically. My, how things do change over time if we are willing to let go, forgive, and forget. My life saving class turned out to be "life saving" in many respects.

Lessons in Life

- Never quit something you really want, as long as it is healthy, reasonable, and prudent.

- Failure can be the best learning experience we can have, especially if it helps us learn priorities in life.

- Learn to let go, forgive, and forget; the benefits outweigh the bitterness many times over.

- Look closely at the potential risk of an effort (I could drown along with the victim) before charging in to be the rescuer (in business as well as in the water).

Action Solutions

- Examine what experiences you have started and then quit. Do you have any regrets about quitting?

  _____

  _____

  _____

- Establish a clear understanding about your feelings toward quitting or losing out (anger, fear, upset, etc.) and determine whether there is immediate action that can be taken to resolve the situation.

  _____

  _____

  _____

- Develop criteria you will use in the future to determine whether to stick with a goal or to bail out.

  _____

  _____

  _____

Adding Insult to Injury

When I graduated from high school in Kiester, Minnesota, I was not a great student, but not a bad student either. I applied to St. Olaf College, perhaps because my cousin went there and one of my older high school heroes also attended there. Without realizing how difficult college could be, I naively assumed that since they accepted me, I would do okay.

During my first college semester, I struggled to get Cs and worried about being able to keep myself off academic probation. On top of that, I had a real "eye-opening" experience with my former high school principal. He had also been my algebra teacher in our small school so he knew me pretty well.

On a return visit for homecoming weekend, I bumped into the principal after the football game. We happened to be walking to the parking lot together and struck up a casual conversation. He asked me what I was doing now that I was out of high school. I spoke up proudly that I was attending St. Olaf College. His casual response was, "Gee, Wes, I didn't think you were college material." Those words still cut straight to the heart as I think about the hurt and embarrassment I felt. At the time, I didn't respond. I think I was conditioned to suppress feelings as a way of protection from further insult and hurt.

Returning to college after that weekend, I was on a mission to prove my critic wrong. He had touched a nerve with his insulting, degrading comment, and I became determined to overcome, rather than succumb, to his expectations. In retrospect, I think his hurtful comment burned a symbolic brand on my brain. On one hand, I would like to be angry and hold a grudge about his comment, on the other hand I have to thank him for the challenge.

Many years later, I can look back and realize that I have two Masters Degrees and two PhDs, and I am certified in Biofeedback, Stress Management, and Sport Psychology. All of this may have come about, in part, because of (not in spite of) my former algebra teacher. Thank you, Mr. Lewis. The lesson you taught me went far beyond the algebra class, and I never again will have to feel embarrassed about my academic performance.

Lessons in Life

- What appears to be a hurtful or an insulting comment may be intended to challenge you to reach higher or to dig deeper to meet a goal you never considered possible.

- Even if a hurtful or insulting comment was malicious, you can transform the negative into a positive challenge for yourself in that situation.

- Discover the driving forces in your life history that seem to help you be successful or that keep you from being successful.

Action Solutions

- Examine an experience you have had in the past that made you uncomfortable or embarrassed. Did you perceive it positively and react in a productive way or did you let it thwart your potential?

- Establish a plan whereby you can anticipate *Doo-Doo* happening. Show how you can be prepared to make the best of any bad situation by restructuring your thinking to always find a way to grow from it.

- List the driving forces in your life that have helped or hurt you.

Cut Your Own Path Through the Chaff

The words of my high school speech teacher, Mr. Farrel, echo in my ears when I stand before an audience. As I seek to build rapport and respect with my audience, I hear his words, "Find out what everyone else is doing...and don't do that. Set yourself apart from the crowd."

In keeping with that challenge, figure out what others are doing (to make themselves happy or miserable), then chart your own course, find another route, march to the tune of your own drummer. You cannot find happiness following someone else's dream.

Whether seeking happiness or success in a career or relationship, it is critically important to remember, as Frank Sinatra sang, "Do it my way." People often ask me, "How did you get where you are today?" These are usually young people struggling to find a career, or adults who are unhappy and searching for a new direction in life. My answer to that question is always the same. I had to get centered, define my priorities, and figure out how "to do it my way." My grandfather told me to find my passion and the money and fame would follow. So when I heard Mr. Farrel say to me, "If you will polish your gift of gab, someday you can make a living with it," I knew I was on the road to my passion and to my future! My grandfather had taught me to be a storyteller and Mr. Farrel taught me, with discipline and effort, that I could polish those storytelling skills into successful effective public speaking!

Regardless what you choose to do in life, be an individual — unique and special — with all your own warts and beauty marks. For me, those unique and special talents led me first into Brahma bull riding (don't try this at home) and other cowboy adventures. From there, I eventually turned to marathon running and the far more challenging and scary task of speaking to thousands of people, young and old, across the country. When I stand in front of a group, whether it be 100 or 1,000 people, I enjoy entertaining people with humorous stories of my own struggles through life. However, what sets me apart from all others in my field is the fact that I try to make people uncomfortable enough with my message and stories that they are motivated into health-enhancing behavior. Thus, helping them to find, as I have, the humor and growth in nearly every challenging experience in life.

The educational reward for being bold, abrasive, and self-deprecating in my humor lies in the quote from one of my seminar participants who said, "Can I buy the T-shirt that says, 'The speaker just jump-started me into action'?" That comment is a treasured compliment. I decided to become a physical educator when I was in the tenth grade. I made that decision based on Mr. Farrel's guidance and my grandfather's encouragement to use my "gift of gab." Thirty years later, I am still teaching and encouraging people to work harder at being healthier and more physically active. It has been as a result of my unique and sometimes abrasive style that I have been fortunate enough to cut my path through the chaff and have created a significant impact in the world around me.

Lessons in Life

- Discover how you are unique, then maximize the potential that exists (in being funny or, insightful, creative or whatever).

- Become aware of the talents, physical characteristics, and experiences with which you have been blessed.

- Make the very best of your gifts and talents by taking on new challenges and celebrating your successes while downplaying the occasional flop.

- Don't skimp on the "hard work" that it takes to refine your talents.
- Listen to the "old folks" (those who are chronologically gifted) in your life. They have great wisdom to offer.

Action Solutions

- List the unique characteristics that "set you apart from others."

_____

_____

_____

- Itemize the ways you can capitalize on your unique characteristics in your personal and professional life.

_____

_____

_____

- Describe one situation where you know you could work harder to make something good happen.

_____

_____

_____

- List the "old folks" in your life who might have some wisdom to share with you.

_____

_____

_____

The Trials of Life Are Intended to Make Us Better—Not Bitter

One of the most devastating events in life is to be rejected. Being terminated from a job you want and need is a rejection that disrupts every aspect of one's personal life. Just hearing the words, "You've been fired" breaks down one's self-concept, more than any other challenge in life. I was twenty-seven years old when I got fired. It was particularly traumatic because it threatened the livelihood of my family. I was in graduate school at the University of Pittsburgh. I lost two jobs and a place to live within a two-week period.

To supplement my meager graduate school earnings, I worked in a newly-built apartment complex in a bartering arrangement. We had living space in the apartment at no cost in return for my hard work at cleaning the laundry room and vacuuming hallways. It was a great situation because I enjoyed the hard physical work and the satisfaction of having a wonderful place to live without paying rent.

In May of 1973, we had two devastating crises occur. First, I found out that I was losing my university assistantship income (a temporary loss for three months over the summer). Shortly thereafter, I was called into the superintendent's office at the apartment complex. I was about to lose the job that covered our rent in the apartment. Within that short time period, it appeared that the world had come crashing down upon us. We had lost all of our income and would not have a place to live. My wife and I were devastated, to say the least, but we didn't have time to wallow in the *Doo-Doo*.

Making **DO** out of **Doo-Doo**

I immediately began calling people who might have some kind of work (hopefully, work that included a place to live for the summer). On my third call, I reached the owner of a travel camp based in Chicago. My wife and I had both worked for him previously as staff counselors in the summers. I asked what seemed to me like a ridiculous question, "Do you have any work available for the summer at this late date?" (It was May fifteenth and summer was only a few weeks away). I was absolutely stunned by his response. He said, "Are you really available for the summer?" My reply was, "Are you kidding, I am so-o-o-o-o available! I have nothing better to do and we have no place to live."

Fortunately for us, one of his trip directors had just had a serious back injury and would not be able to travel or work that summer. Not only did he have jobs for me and my wife, but it included free living accommodations on a sailboat in the Caribbean Islands. We spent that summer, and the following summer in the Caribbean, and made more money than we ever expected. At the same time, I developed valuable management experience and new interpersonal conflict resolution skills. The irony is that this wonderful job experience of sailing and scuba diving in the Caribbean would never have happened if I hadn't been fired and feeling desperate. This is a classic example of how we *Made Do out of Doo-Doo.*

Since that time, I have been released (or fired) from three other part-time work-related ventures. In each case, I was upset when it occurred, but later was able to turn the bitterness into energy and had the perseverance to bounce back. Ironically, as I reflect on each of those big disappointments, I find that I am better off as a result of each setback, partly because I was fortunate enough to stumble into several other wonderful opportunities. Obviously, I did have to struggle for a period of time after the hammer came down, but it prompted me to make appropriate changes in my life (i.e., going back to school, seeking new ventures, and becoming more determined or resourceful).

Whenever I share my experience of losing a job (as a sample of real life stress) with seminar participants, I am routinely met with numerous other stories of serious professional or financial catastrophes (e.g., declaring bankruptcy). In most of these cases, the individuals survived the loss without serious problems, and the outcome five years later was always positive. Many people find a wonderful opportunity through a career change that might never have occurred without having lost an existing job.

Lessons in Life

- Getting fired or being upset by some catastrophe could be the best thing that might happen to you.
- Grieve, momentarily, about the loss, but then move on with your life without delay.
- Roll with the punches, ride out the bumps in the road, make lemonade out of lemons, *Make Do out of Doo-Doo,* and develop a sense of hardiness for living.
- Be open and honest about your situation with friends, relatives, and professional associates who may be able to help you cope with your set-back and find some solution.

Action Solutions

- List the lessons in life you have learned or how you have bene-fitted from a "bitter" experience in the past.

_____

_____

- Practice talking about a loss or disappointment, even if it was years ago and you think you have gotten past it.

_____

_____

- If you are currently dealing with a loss or disappointment, write it out so you can see what is reality and what is not.

_____

_____

Friends Are Important, But Pay Attention to Your Enemies

Most of us have some special relationships with friends who we have known for a long time, and we tend to nourish our friendships. The question is, how do we cope with the actions and words of our critics and enemies?

Would you believe it is very possible to learn a lot from your critics? Are they truly hateful and vindictive for no apparent reason, or are they just trying to give you information and feedback you hadn't yet considered? Does paranoia and/or anger always have to follow criticism? When was the last time you were feeling victimized by a nasty colleague or overzealous competitor? These are important questions and concerns that each of us have dealt with from time to time.

In the mid 80s, as a fireball, high energy, impatient, professional working in state government, I let my passion for action be heard whenever and wherever possible. Without realizing the impact of my voice in community service, I inadvertently caused several people to lose their volunteer service appointments on a highly visible governor-appointed committee. Those displaced committee members were very unhappy and one influential person, in particular, used his connections to retaliate against me in a vigorous campaign designed to sully my reputation across the country.

Needless to say, I was shocked and surprised to learn later that I had made some very big enemies by simply trying to do what I thought was right. My lesson in life, about paying attention to your enemies, occurred while at an international meeting of prestigious health promotion professionals in Canada.

At the conference, much to my chagrin, the program chair, a man named Jim who I did not know personally, began to exhibit hostile behavior toward me. He would not speak to me directly or acknowledge any of my contributions during the course of the five-day meeting. My frustration and anxiety reached an all-time high when we were randomly thrown together as partners in one of the closing "team-building" activities.

Jim and I were directed to construct a plaster mask on each other's faces and then symbolically decorate the mask. As Jim applied the wet plaster strips to my face; I could sense the tension and discomfort he felt being my partner and touching my face. Doing this activity, without verbal interaction, allowed me a great deal of time to contemplate the fact that Jim apparently hated me even though he did not know me personally. Lying still without speaking for 45 minutes with Jim standing overhead made me contemplate how it is that someone becomes your enemy. How does hate unfold? What brought this on and how could I resolve it?

After the plaster mask was removed from my face, I subsequently performed the same ritual on Jim. Because of my discomfort with the tension that existed between the two of us, I could hold back no longer and blurted out, "Jim, we have to talk."

Over the next four hours of mask-making and decorating, he finally opened up enough to share the fact that he had been influenced by a good friend who was one of the Nebraska Gubernatorial Committee members who had been displaced. His anger originated from his belief that my actions (back in Nebraska) had resulted in the ousting of his good friend. He also believed my actions were intended to gain personal power and recognition. Wow! As I sank into a state of disbelief, it became apparent to me how easily my impatience and bold actions could be misinterpreted.

"Ready, fire, aim" has been my motto for years with great success, but this time it had "backfired." My enemy was providing me with a valuable lesson about tact, hurt, mistrust, patience, and greed. How appropriate that, while removing our masks, we had discovered our actual selves. After our conversation, Jim and I walked along a scenic path, masks in hand. We agreed that we needed to bury the hatchet and, as result, we "buried our masks." My lesson in life was that I now pay almost as much attention to my enemies as I do to my friends. Whenever I sense a level of tension in the air, I try to make opportunities to bring closure to the unfinished business and, if necessary, find a way to "bury the hatchet."

Lessons in Life

- Pay attention to your critics and enemies. They may help you see habit patterns that need to be changed.

- Express your emotions about the effect the anger or hostility is having on you. If you don't let it out, the effect could be harmful to your health.

- Suggest a course of action to resolve conflicts. Learn to express what you need or feel.

Action Solutions

- Describe a situation in which you have inadvertently offended someone.

_____

_____

- Describe a personal experience where you or someone else has been successful in bringing a difficult interpersonal conflict to a satisfactory conclusion by communicating directly and sincerely.

_____

_____

- Prepare a script of what you might say to a person with whom you have had some personal conflict recently or in the past. Give the person the benefit of the doubt regarding his/her misdeeds while also considering your own shortcomings surrounding the conflict.

_____

_____

When Bad Things Happen to Good People

Rolly was one of my clients in biofeedback therapy who had developed multiple sclerosis after years of high pressure farming decisions. His stress was compounded so much by social discomfort, that just being around other people (beyond family) made him very uncomfortable. He would say, "I just get all nerved up around people."

Many years before I began working with Rolly, his physician had prescribed Valium to help him be more relaxed. Rolly thought it was great stuff—he took a lot of it over the years. I have to wonder whether the onset of Rolly's MS was just coincidental with his long history of stress and over-aggressive use of the tranquilizer. Regardless, Rolly tried everything possible to battle his symptoms. It has been a long slow period of degeneration for him and he has lost most of his voluntary functioning.

His early symptoms of MS began to develop when his two sons were teenagers. As a result, he needed their assistance with the farming operation even more than usual because of his own fatigue, shakiness, and poor vision. Ironically, his kids seemed to thrive on the unexpected demand for their time and effort. As I observed this family struggle for many years with the complications surrounding Rolly's MS, it was apparent that both of these teenagers grew up quickly and became solid, responsible young men well before their age of maturity. For example, they seemed to be unaffected by the usual temptations of teenage smoking, alcohol use, or pranks that beset other teens in the community. It seemed as though they were preoccupied by the sense of responsibility thrust upon them by their father's illness.

In the process of carrying out important tasks and making difficult decisions, Rolly's kids were blessed with the feeling of being "grown up." Kids benefit greatly from the sense of being needed and appreciated by adults. Both boys and their younger sister heard many sincere comments of appreciation expressed by their parents and other family/community members for the extraordinary circumstances they were handling. That is, they were gradually taking over the farming as their father's health deteriorated. Obviously, the challenge of meeting those expectations was very exciting and probably enriched their lives. Ironically, we know (from other research) that kids who feel valued and appreciated are less likely to make dumb decisions about sex, drugs, and alcohol.

The bottom line is that my client Rolly was able to look upon his own illness (MS) as a "crazy kind of mixed blessing" whereby his kids benefitted greatly from the need to take over the farm. The reason this example has such great significance is that Rolly has come to realize that, prior to his illness, he was a hard guy to get along with, and his kids might have been driven off the farm by his hard-driving management style. While the illness for Rolly has been extremely difficult and has caused the family undue sadness and disruption, this family is a living example of *Making Do out of Doo-Doo.* The family's strong moral and religious beliefs made it possible for them to find something good in a bad situation.

Lessons in Life

- Bad things do happen to good people. What is important is how we recover from these events and whether we grow stronger as a result.

- Giving kids important tasks and opportunities is helpful in developing their sense of self-worth and their desire to be successful.

- Providing lots of encouragement and appreciation for extraordinary efforts by kids is very helpful in keeping them on them on track and safe.

- Accepting the consequences of bad things (such as medical illness) can be easier if we can find a coincidental positive outcome.

Action Solutions

- Review the variety of "bad things" that may have happened to you and your family. Pick one or more of these in which you can identify unexpected positive outcomes that occurred amidst the distress.

_____

_____

_____

- Condition yourself to expect potential challenges in life and prepare a backup plan or contingencies that you might fall back on as a cushion to protect yourself from disappointment, loss, etc.

_____

_____

_____

- Make a list of statements of encouragement or appreciation that you would like to offer to your kids or other important people in your life.

_____

_____

_____

Finding the G.O.W.N. in Your Life

For almost every hurt in life, there is a support group. Through Alcoholics Anonymous, Weight Watchers, Gamblers Anonymous, and many other traditional support group activities, we have learned the power and value of "social support." I am fortunate to have an informal support group of my own that I call the Good Ole' Woman's Network (G.O.W.N. support system). My husband has often said an eight-minute phone call to one of my close friends is a wise use of our long distance dollars. The chance to vent, ask questions, seek guidance, discuss professional and family issues, and always have a giggle, proves to be powerful therapy. I am comfortable sharing anything with people in my G.O.W.N. because of the human qualities of its members. They are honest, caring, trustworthy, dependable, compassionate, and optimistic. In addition, however, they have the ability to shake things up and make me face reality.

One of my major adult traumas was facing the reality of being dismissed from a job I loved. For nineteen years, I put my heart and soul into improving health and physical education opportunities for children. One Thursday afternoon, upper management summoned me to the "big office." During that meeting, they outlined their issues of concern and informed me they would proceed with a fact finding mission aimed at dismissing me. After leaving the office, I drove home to seek solace from the front line general in my G.O.W.N. (my husband, Red). He listened to my story, read the information in the papers I had been given, held me while I sobbed, and repeatedly reassured me, "this will all work out and you will be fine."

The months of legal jockeying dragged on. Due to the suspension, I had plenty of time to spare. One day, I took a horseback ride with another member of my G.O.W.N. The events that followed proved to be my "ah ha!" As Trudy and I proceeded down a scenic trail in the early morning hours, I began lamenting my sob story, my "woe is me" stuff. Trudy listened patiently as she rode along and finally stopped me in my tracks at a wide spot in the trail. She turned her horse 180 degrees to face me directly and said, "Jo, what is it with you? You could have five jobs by tomorrow morning. Why would you fight to work with people who don't want you?" My reply was, "It's the principle, Trudy...the whole thing and how it has been handled is not right!" She replied, "Principle, sminciple...right, wrong! Get a grip. Settle with those folks and get on with your life. While you are haggling about keeping this job, you are not crusading for healthier kids. Get back on task, let it go! Now get back into enjoying this ride."

That day was a new beginning. As the sun peeked through the trees, I saw the light. My lawyer settled the dispute. I resigned with reputation and ego intact, and within twenty-four hours I was employed by a national organization. I had a different employer, but the same crusade. It's my job to ensure that children have every opportunity for healthier and more active lives, and it doesn't matter who gets the recognition.

Trudy and many other woman are a part of my G.O.W.N. for support when needed. They are special people who have a unique combination of human qualities. However, this is not a gender-based support group. There are men in my G.O.W.N. who will listen unconditionally and offer advice where needed. Individuals like Shep, Darrel, Gary, John, Wes, Ron, Phil and my husband, Red, help with periodic "ah ha's!" while sharing my hurts, happiness, and an occasional giggle about life's adventures.

Women tend to seek support and commiseration more than men. There is no need to make it gender specific. Crossing the lines of brothers, uncles, sisters, aunts, and other very good friends, of both genders, is desirable to have a balanced perspective. Otherwise, woman are simply replicating the traditional "good ol' boys network" and that is not healthy or appropriate.

I don't have to be in touch with these people every day, but the fact I know they are there for me is reassuring and comforting. I encourage each of you to seek and find those people who are your G.O.W.N. in life.

Lessons in Life

- It is important to develop a network of individuals to help you with the celebrations and agonies of life.
- Look for the qualities you admire in people, and those qualities could be the foundation of your G.O.W.N. membership.
- Stay in touch with your G.O.W.N. because of your sincere interest in them as well as in maintaining the network.
- Listen to their advice and selectively choose options that get you moving forward.

Actions Solutions

- Make a list of the qualities you value highly and list people you know who possess those qualities.

_____

_____

_____

_____

_____

- Make a list of the people who will be in your G.O.W.N. for the future.

_____

_____

_____

_____

_____

- Describe a time when a member of your G.O.W.N. has given you comfort and advice.

_____

_____

_____

_____

Postscript: I am reminded by my co-author, that many of the men in our society are not inclined to open up and communicate with a network of friends. Ironically, he says, "It is even more important that men develop a network of special people in addition to their spouse and significant others." In his experience as a counselor to hundreds of men and women, Wes says that most men are very good at talking sports, fishing, hunting, politics, and business, but many are reluctant to share more intimate, personal details of their successes and embarrassments. Therefore, we strongly recommend good friendships and support groups where men can practice a special sort of bonding that includes openness and intimacy in communication.

Humor is the Lotion for the Sunburns of Life

Those people who appear to be the happiest usually find any excuse to laugh. Often, when you least expect it, the funniest things can even happen in stressful situations.

On one of my many airplane rides, I experienced a major stress and a rather humorous event. I was seated in the First Class section, seat 2C, on a Boeing 737 (the last seat available on the airplane, someone had to take it). To my right, in seat 2D, was a man turned sideways and looking out the window. In front of me, in seat 1C, was a mother with a ten-month-old baby. The man did not appear as if he wanted to talk so I talked, cooed, and laughed with the baby. We endured the flight safety review, a bumpy ride down the runway during takeoff, and then were airborne.

During the first few minutes of the flight all seemed routine. Then we must have hit some strange turbulence which caused the plane to bounce around a lot. People were complaining and the baby's cooing and laughter changed to tears. Suddenly, the baby had a gastrointestinal reaction to the turbulence that was explosive. She vomited her last feeding directly on my lap. She couldn't have aimed her shot better if she had tried.

Included with the vomit that came hurtling over the seat at me was the child's pacifier. The vomit (grape juice and pancake bits) stuck to my legs and the pacifier bounced into 2D's personal space. The pacifier had landed right between the guy's legs. I was frantically trying to get the gunk off my slacks while thinking to myself, "I wish the kid would quit wailing. Maybe if she had her pacifier she would calm down a bit." I tried to get the gentleman's attention. Things like "Mister, excuse me, Mister. Yoo-hoo, Sir," went unheeded. He would not look at me. One would think the odor would have been more than sufficient to get his attention. I just needed him to reach between his legs, get that pacifier, and give it back to the kid.

What seemed like hours was probably only minutes, but I decided enough time had passed; I was going after the pacifier. I did one last look-see to make sure I knew exactly where to pluck. I extended my arm, fingers ready for the careful grasp, and we hit another air pocket. The turbulence slammed my hand into the guy's privates (crotch). Guess who now turned and glowered at me?

The only thing I could think to say was, "You'll never believe this, Mister, but I'm after a pacifier." The statement was concise and true, but I'm sure he thought I was just groping him. Without uttering a word, he turned and stared out the window again. At that point I decided to let this become the mother's problem. I poked the mother and said, "I can't get it. You'll need to call the flight attendant." The flight attendant responded to the mom's flight call button (she should not have been up, it was much too dangerous). The mother said, "We believe there is a pacifier back there between that guy's legs." The flight attendant reached across me and tapped the man in 2D on the shoulder and said, "Excuse me, sir, we're trying to verify if there's a pacifier between your legs."

Amidst all the confusion, disturbance, and stress of this situation, there was also humor. The requests and questions directed at 2D were correct and concise communication, but they could have been misinterpreted. Of course, we retrieved the pacifier and calmed the baby. I made no further attempts to chat with 2D. We ended up landing safely.

There could have been deep *Doo-Doo* if 2D had complained to the airline or sued me. During the confusion while attempting to retrieve the pacifier, I became very tense due to what I perceived to be a very stressful situation. Since then, I can now laugh out loud and enjoy the story resulting from this unlikely chain of events, but there are several lessons to be learned from this story.

Lessons in Life

- Think about the situation before you speak; your remarks could be interpreted differently than you intended them.

- Realize that some people's sense of urgency may not be as intense as yours.

- Try to find humor in the aftermath of stressful events but recognize that what you may think is hilarious may not be funny to another person.

Action Solutions

- Describe a situation where what you said or did was misinterpreted.

_____

_____

_____

- What changes in your communication style do you need to make in order to insure that your message is clearly understood?

_____

_____

_____

- Give an example of a stressful situation that you have been able to defuse by using some form of humor.

_____

_____

_____

If Your Horse is Dead... Dismount

On one of my many trips, I rushed off one airplane to make a connection and left my Atlanta Commemorative Leather Olympic Ski Jacket in the overhead bin by mistake. It was an expensive item and a very special gift that I treasured. The gate agent at my connecting flight called the cabin cleaning staff who reported they had the jacket and would send it to me. I handed the gate agent my card, $10 for mailing, and headed home. Two months later the jacket still had not arrived and I was very upset. Every time I put on a different jacket I was reminded of my loss and the jacket began taking on more value to me in its absence. I thought bad things about the airline employee who stole (I was sure it was not misplaced) my jacket, and I was also angry with myself for leaving the jacket behind in the first place.

I had nothing but "should haves" in my mind: I should have remembered it; I should have gone back to get it; I should have complained to the president of the airline. All my thoughts were focused on the loss, instead of moving on with life. I wrote letters, made phone calls, and even tried to visit the lost and found warehouse.

I now realize the time and energy I put into stewing about getting the jacket back was an effort in futility. It was not life or death and I do have other jackets. I made a mistake by leaving it on the airplane in a rush, and, in the long term, this loss should not have been very high on my worry/upset list. There are so-o-o-o-o many other more important things in my life.

I finally worked through all the negative thoughts and the wasted energy spent on the jacket as I sat in a hospital room waiting for the biopsy reports from my husband's colon surgery. In those moments of shuddering fear, I realized how ridiculous it was for me to be upset about a little ol' jacket. How could I let myself become upset by a material item? I needed a reminder to give thanks for what I did have and let the jacket go. It's gone! The colon cancer surgery and the well-being of my husband were so much more important. I hoped that someone who needed a jacket for warmth was wearing that awesome item with great appreciation. For me the message was, "Let it go." If your horse is dead...Dismount!

Red's prognosis is great. The jacket is gone and so is the cancer. I definitely know which of those is the most important. There are many other personal and professional hurts and losses I have experienced over the years that received far more attention than they deserved. Grieve the loss as much as might be appropriate, then move ahead with an action plan that might result in some outcome or product that exceeds that which you have lost. Other chapters in the book ("The Trials of Life Are Intended to Make Us Better—Not Bitter," "Establish a Spirit of Living and Hardiness," "The Purple Sweater," and "Everyone's Allowed an Occasional Failure") provide examples of ways in which we can face difficult circumstances and *Make Do out of Doo-Doo* by moving on with life with a new layer of hardiness.

Lessons in Life

- Stay focused and keep your head on straight—rushing to catch a plane (or some other urgency) might cause more mistakes and resultant stress than the "rushing" was worth.

- Be more deliberate about taking charge and follow-up more promptly.

- Once it is gone—let it go—move on to better things. This is hard to do but it is so very important.

- Learn to forgive and wish the best for others who might be in greater need.

- Family and health take priority over "stuff and things."

Action Solutions

- Recall issues, events or happenings that you wish you could forget and just move beyond. Do an inventory of all those you can remember.

_____

_____

_____

- If you still have things you need to "let go of," recognize the time, energy, and fussing that you have already wasted on the issue and set a plan to move ahead.

_____

_____

_____

- Set a plan to catch yourself in advance of the next occurrence where you might be tempted to over-react to an inevitable loss.

_____

_____

_____

Mind Your Manners, Please

I witnessed the epitome of rudeness during one of my travel excursions. As I stood at the customer service counter sorting out my travel options after missing a connecting flight, a man "blew" through the doorway and "charged" up to the counter. As he flopped his hanging bag and tried to unload his other luggage, he knocked me sideways away from the counter. While I was trying to recover my balance, he plopped his day planner onto the counter and started his demands for service.

The Service Concierge, Connie, and I were amazed at his rudeness. He talked fast, loud, and never presented a complete thought. When he finally took a breath, Connie said, "Excuse me sir," but he started talking again. "Sir," she said, but he kept babbling. "Sir, Sir" (he's still talking...and demanding). After her fourth attempt to explain something to him, he blurted out. "Don't you know who I am?"

She put up her index finger (as if to say "ah ha!") and went directly to the phone. Her words on the phone were, "Is this Security? Good! I have a man here who does not know who he is. You do better with those issues than I do. I'll try to keep him here and you hurry over so we can help him figure out who he is." She calmly hung up, looked up at him, and he quieted down instantly and became a slightly more reasonable customer.

I am amazed when people display a complete lack of manners and, also, at how we are so tolerant of rudeness and poor manners. Sometime later, as I reflected on how rude this traveler had been, I considered whether there had been times that I may have been perceived as rude because I was in a hurry. Much to my dismay, I realized it had happened not long ago. I thought about an incident in a computer store when I was in a hurry to buy a memory chip for my computer.

My nephew and I were shopping for just one item that day and I felt rushed to get home to finish other urgent tasks. I told the young man behind the counter what I needed, he took it out of the security case, and then the ordeal began. I was primed with cash to avoid the credit card hassle. But he started asking me a bunch of irrelevant questions: "What is your full name, mailing address, date of birth, type and brand of computer? What other electronic gadgets do you have in your household?" And the questions just went on and on. I interrupted to ask, "Why can't I just pay cash for the item, get my receipt, and go? I am in a big hurry."

He slowly and methodically informed me that he needed all this information so he could expedite service the next time I came in. I tried to explain, "I'm am just visiting in this town and probably won't be back. I need this memory now, please hurry." He said, "But ma'am, you don't understand. I can't finish the sale without getting all this information." By this time, my impatience had totally embarrassed my nephew who works for the same computer chain in his hometown. My curtness and many protesting comments had delayed the process causing the clerk to be upset, and I still did not have the computer chip!

I took another deep breath and said to the young man, "Please make up something after I'm out of here. Fill in the blanks on your computer screen now and I promise not to come back. Please, can I pay for this memory chip and go?" He looked at me as if my elevator did not go all the way to the top, nodded calmly, and said, "That will be $46.11 please." I gave him a fifty-dollar bill and said, "Keep the change and buy yourself lunch." As I proceeded to the door, my nephew had long since distanced himself from the counter as he was getting more embarrassed by the moment.

I suddenly realized that the rudeness of the man at the airport was no more abrasive than my behavior in the computer store. Because I travel so much, I encounter lots of folks in the "service industry." Most of them are trying to do the best they can, sometimes under very difficult circumstances. Perhaps if we all were more considerate and patient, we would be less stressed, more happy, and healthy.

During the long drive home that day, my nephew and I had several conversations about this event. The first was hard because I had suspected he was not comfortable with the way I reacted to the clerk. Each time we brought it up again, we found more humor in the situation. I finally concluded that "I was not the brightest crayon in the box" in kindergarten, so what did he expect. That made him chuckle and soothed the ruffled feathers of a sensitive teenager.

Lessons in Life

- "Mind your manners" and "please and thank you" still go a long way in helping get what you want/need.
- Teach your children well. Model by example and have the courage to acknowledge your rudeness and apologize when you are not a shining example of "minding your manners."
- Practice, practice, practice. Treat people like you want to be treated and greet them like you want to be greeted.

Action Solutions

- Reflect on a recent incident where you lost it, where you "just melted down," and were rude and obnoxious without any good reason.

_____

_____

- If someone treated you as rudely as you may have been treated, how angry would you be?

_____

- What can you do to ensure you will mind your manners in the future?

_____

_____

Holler If You Need Something

Coming from a farm and ranch background, I seem to encounter many unique individuals whose life stories produce lasting and meaningful *lessons in life*. July 2, 1998 was the final resting day for a cowboy's cowboy named David A. Martin. He lived to be eighty-three years old and was married to the same woman for sixty-one years. I'm sure he drank and smoked too much, ate foods high in fat, made other unhealthy choices, and yet still lived a long and full life by most standards.

So before you discount any of the contents of the chapters on nutrition, alcohol, safety, cardiovascular activity, tobacco, sleep, etc. let's move right into the fact that he probably inherited a great set of genes. Maybe if the rest of us could trade our parents for his, while also practicing health-enhancing behaviors, we might live well beyond his eighty-three years. This story, however, is not to find fault with Dave about his habits, but to describe the dramatic impact he had on other peoples' lives.

Dave was known as a horse trader and you either loved or hated him. Most of the huge congregation gathered on that July day will remember his empathy and generosity. You could borrow anything from Dave and everyone knew of his great spirit. What many did not know was the story that his grandson disclosed in his eulogy. He told how two young boys became a part of the Martin family.

One day while baling hay next to an orphanage, Dave noticed a young boy standing at the edge of the field. After the third time around the field, the young boy was still there. Dave never met a stranger he didn't like, so naturally he got off the tractor and went to talk with the boy. After a few minutes of conversation, the young boy bluntly asked Dave if he could go home with him. This cowboy must have had a heart of gold because he made an instant decision that the young boy was going to become a part of the Martin family.

Remember that Dave was a horse trader by profession, so he had no difficulty convincing his wife and the orphanage administrator that taking the boy into his home was a very good deal for everybody. But the story doesn't end there. A few years later, Dave observed another young boy standing at the edge of that same field. This young boy was crying, so Dave stopped on his first trip around the field to inquire about the tears. Yes, you guessed it. The young man had courage enough to ask if he could go home with Dave that day.

In addition to their five biological children, Dave and Bonnie gave new life to these two young orphan boys. Both those young men and their families were in the pews as we let go and allowed the cowboy's cowboy to go to the "big hay field in the sky." These two families are a living legacy of the tremendous impact this cowboy's cowboy had in this world and that is why he will be remembered fondly.

That story during the funeral service caused me to get tears in my eyes and reflect on Dave's most recent act of kindness to Red and me. As my husband was getting ready for his third major surgery in two months, I called Dave to update him on Red's "medical moments" (that's my description for his prognosis, "live or die," because these are not "memorable or precious moments"). He closed the conversation as he often did with, "If you need something just holler." In my experience people often say that, but not many actually mean it. Not many folks step forward and actually make themselves available to help out just because they know it is needed.

Around the time of Red's surgery, one of my longhorn cows (Tex) kept getting her horns wedged in the hay feeder and she was unable to get free. The other cows would poke her with their horns as they went by (trust me that hurts) and she was beginning to dehydrate from lack of water. Red had asked that I not leave the hospital but I had this cow problem that worried me and so entered Dave Martin, the cowboy's cowboy. Knowing full well that my presence by Red's side was as important to the healing process as anything the surgeon had done, I reached out for help. Remembering his words ("just holler"), I called Dave and asked if he would rescue Tex and take her back to his place. Dave and his son Davie Jr. freed Tex from the hay feeder, took her home to their place, and returned her two months later, healthier and more content than I could have ever expected. When I drove to Dave and Bonnie's with check in hand, I asked, "What do I owe you?" His response was "Ah shucks, don't worry about it. We'll figure it out and I'll get even with ya' sometime." He never accepted any payment for taking care of Tex or other favors he did during Red's prolonged illness.

Later, when it was Dave's last days in the hospital, I went by to give him a back rub. He would smile, wink, and then go back to sleep. Shortly after that, he died peacefully in his sleep. I'm not sure if we are "even" Dave, but your family members (and all the others I care about in this way) can sure "holler if they need something." Knowing him has changed my life. Dave Martin is definitely one of those unique people whose life story carries on through me and others who have been touched by these meaningful "lessons in life."

Lessons in Life

- If you offer assistance, be there and do it without being told exactly what to do. Show a little initiative to know what needs to be done and do it.

- Consider if the way you offer assistance conveys a sense of sincerity. If your gesture is frivolous — it will be very apparent to others.

- When you are in need, are you comfortable asking friends or relatives for help?

- Develop strong relationships so that people would consider it a privilege to be able to help you out.

- If we told stories about you at the end of your life span, would people be touched by your life story?

Action Solutions

- Describe how you want to be remembered by others.

_____

_____

_____

- What could you be doing that shows more caring and giving?

_____

_____

_____

- List the things you are doing now that you would want to be your legacy to the others who might know you after you are gone?

_____

_____

_____

Driving with Del

Are there lessons in life to be learned from a dying man? Stories from movies and books portray numerous examples to ponder, but it becomes far more poignant when we experience these lessons personally. In the late summer of 1998, my neighbor called to let me know that his lung cancer had reappeared and had metastasized to other parts of his body. His treatment options had run out and death was imminent. The news was very startling and, of course, it accelerated our efforts at being "a good neighbor." Naturally, we offered to help with feeding the horses, cleaning the barn, and other "chores" that needed to be done when you live on an acreage. However, what Del needed more than anything was help in coping with his fear of dying. It became apparent that when you are really, really sick you also have a lot of time on your hands to think.

One day my friend Trudy and I were agonizing over the fact that we might soon be losing our good buddy, Del. We asked him if he wanted to go for a horse and buggy ride and he was delighted. Del's health had deteriorated such that his horseback riding and cattle roping days were over. Bottled oxygen was a necessary "carry along" on his activities of daily living, so the buggy ride seemed like the only viable mode of transportation for the retired cowboy and his friends.

As Trudy and Del ambled along in the buggy and I rode alongside on my horse just like we were out on another cowboy adventure, we talked about horses, cows, the weather, the crops, and my peacocks (they would occasionally stray to Del and Pat's house for gourmet meals). As the conversation progressed, Del struggled for his next breath of air. I realized we could be taking Del's last buggy ride (he died just a few months later).

About a week after the buggy ride, Del showed up at our house for a visit. I think he really appreciated the time we spent with him knowing the end was near. He and my husband, Red, sat on the couch and engaged in "cowboy talk." In all that conversation not much had been mentioned about Del's illness and especially about his impending demise. Then, after a brief coughing spell, he looked at Red and said, "Red, I really don't want to die." It became unusually quiet as Red and I both searched for words to fill the empty air. Red, who is particularly strong in his own faith, uttered, "But Del, you're going to a better place." At which point Del immediately countered with, "Lots of people have been telling me that Red, but," he said, "I've got to tell you, Red, I don't see anything wrong with this place I'm in right now. I really don't want to leave."

The conversation came to a full stop for what seemed like hours, but was really only minutes. I am sure Del was pondering the thoughts about his own death, but for Red and me, it was a real "wake-up call" about our own lives. After Del left, we talked about the important things in life that we might have been over-looking. For example, I often ask participants in my workshops, "If you knew that you only had a few months to live, how would you spend your time differently?" They always swallow hard and laugh just a little when I remind them that patients who are on their deathbed rarely say, "I wish I had spent more time at the office or at work."

Red and I talked about such questions as, "Would you rather die suddenly or would you prefer having the time to plan, as occurs with a terminal illness?" While we found no obvious answer to these questions, it did make us ponder for a moment and pledge to each other that we would try to live each day as if it were our last together. Even now, as Red and I bring our business and pleasure activities to a close at the end of each day…we still behave as if it could be our "last buggy ride."

When we attended Del's funeral in late November, we observed a powerful ceremony (all pre-planned by Del) celebrating his life. Humor was imbedded in the eulogy, as Del would have wanted it. In one example of the humor, Del's stepdaughter, Caren, shared one of her fondest memories as she felt an especially close bond with him. It seems that when she was in middle school, Del would let her put make-up and jewelry on him to see how it looked. Not surprisingly, the congregation broke into uproarious laughter when the minister added that Del never did the jewelry and make-up thing when his cowboy friends were around.

I was reminded of a more serious lesson in life when I heard the minister say that Del stopped expressing his fear of dying near the end as his faith grew stronger. Even though he appeared to be physically weaker, he came across as more powerful and reassured about the future as he seemed to have resolved his concerns about death.

Lessons in Life

- Tobacco use is health debilitating. Don't use it.
- Take care of business while you're healthy. Make sure others know about finances, wills, your wishes, family heirlooms, etc.
- The unknown is fearful but isn't most of life about unknowns?
- Faith becomes our rock when we have no experiences from which to gain strength, guidance, and wisdom.
- Even in the most solemn circumstances, humor is essential; it helps us become more accepting of inevitable losses in life.

Action Solutions

- Are you a smoker?   ☐ Yes ☐ No
  - If yes, do you want to quit?   ☐ Yes ☐ No
- Now consider that you must quit and describe how you might do that.

_____

_____

_____

_____

_____

Making **DO** out of **Doo-Doo**

- Are you living in a way that you want to be remembered?

_____

_____

_____

  - If not, what are you going to do differently?

    _____

    _____

    _____

- Describe how you live your life with the full range of emotions inclusive of humor and seriousness.

_____

_____

_____

Come On Baby, Light My Fire

All the major role models who influenced my life were smokers. These were the same people who taught me about manners, love, giving, truth, honesty, and respect for all but particularly your elders. Therefore, whatever these folks did or said, in my view, must be okay. With all the great lessons in life they had taught me, I was attracted to almost every habit they exhibited, thus came my first encounter with tobacco use.

As a kid, I knew to steal their cigarettes would have been wrong. Therefore, I needed to find some other way to try this "cool thing" called smoking. My first attempt was to ask my Grandpa Earl if I could try his cigarette. He immediately denied my request and told me smoking was an awful, nasty, dirty habit. Now that confused me; Grandpa Earl was a cool guy and I didn't think he would do awful, nasty, dirty things. As a result, I was still fascinated with what the adults were doing with that smoky, smelly thing hanging out of their mouths. I decided I would try to be just like Grandpa, Mom, and Dad.

I found a corn cob pipe and matches and embarked on my first smoking adventure. My little brother and I were pretty good buddies so it seemed logical to include him in the experience. We took off to the pasture armed with pipe, matches, and determination. As we sat in the middle of the pasture pondering our next step, I discovered we were missing the essential ingredient, tobacco. So now what? What do we smoke? It was a long trip back to the house, so I looked around and the answer was right under our noses.

Dried cow poop (cow chips) looked surprisingly like to-bacco. I put the cow chip on a big rock, mashed it up with an-other rock, and sure enough it resembled the stuff that grandpa rolled into his filterless cigarettes. I poked the pipe full of mashed cow chips and proceeded to light it. Being a nice older sister, I allowed my brother the honor of the first puff. He cried, coughed, and developed a full-fledged asthma attack. How-ever, my concern for his well being was overwhelmed by my cu-riosity about smoking. I was sure Dick was a wimp. I would show him how to do this smoking thing. After three big puffs, I, too, began coughing, choking, gasping, and tearing. Then the vomiting commenced! That marked the end of my smoking ca-reer.

Over the years, I have concluded that my adult role models were nuts if they thought smoking was great. I knew I loved them, but I am still amazed and confused about their smoking behavior. The so-called smoking enjoyment zapped the quality and quantity of their life. Toward the end of my granddad and my stepfather's lives, they suffered the same kind of coughing, choking, tearing, and even vomiting. Ironically, these were the same symptoms that my brother Dick and I had experienced as children in that pasture forty-five years before, however, theirs were caused by emphysema. They would gasp for breath and even vomit as they tried desperately to breathe in the last few years before they died. Remarkably, neither Dick nor I ever be-came tobacco smokers. Outlining the hazards of tobacco use for readers would be futile. Neither Dick nor I abstained from to-bacco because of the awful, painful deaths of our relatives. Rather, we were powerfully influenced by a single nauseous ex-perience with cow poop tobacco!

Is it surprising that many of the tobacco prevention educa-tion efforts targeted at children and youth have been unsuccess-ful? All around them, today's youth see smoking portrayed as cool, sophisticated, and mature. Therefore, as my brother and I discovered so many years ago, maybe it is time for a more radi-cal approach. Can't you envision the new biology lab experi-ment featuring "cow chips" burning?

Lessons in Life

- The jury is in and it appears that tobacco "leads the pack" for its cause/effect relationships with heart disease and lung cancer.
- Tobacco is addictive and we must be gentle with those trying to kick their addiction, but we must try harder to decrease the number of tobacco users.
- If you're trying to quit smoking, know that it will be a struggle.
- If we offered up dried cow poop instead of tobacco and then said, "Come on baby, light my fire," we might have fewer teenage smokers.

Action Solutions

- If you are a tobacco user, what lessons in life do you need to work on so you can STOP?

_____

_____

_____

- If you are not a smoker, but you have friends and loved ones who are smoking, what are you doing to help someone else break the habit and start being more healthy and productive?

_____

_____

- If you still use tobacco, what could you do to reduce or eliminate the usage for your health sake and that of your family?

_____

_____

_____

Prohibition Ain't the Answer

Sixty-five years ago during the years of prohibition, we tried eliminating intoxicating beverages and it didn't work. Alcohol is one of the few *legal* intoxicating drugs. It is used socially, and in moderation, by a large percentage of the population. A growing number of people have difficulty in controlling their consumption.

Alice is one who admits to being an alcoholic. Perhaps these are some of the factors that tipped her in the direction of abuse instead of moderate use. She grew up learning by observing to be very cautious and careful about expressing emotions. Her staunch and conservative family taught that you should not say anything bad about people or express your true feelings. Her fear was that any direct expression of anger or frustration might hurt someone's feelings or somehow tarnish the good name and reputation of the family. As a result, she learned to suppress her own feelings while trying to please others as much as possible. In addition, her parental family did not consume alcohol at any time during her child and adolescent years.

In Alice's childhood there were no open conflicts, arguments, or confrontations. Her mother was widowed early in life and became the matriarch of the family who no one questioned. This very hard-working, conscientious, tough grandma adapted quickly to challenges throughout her life. Therefore, while she did not like making decisions for the family, everyone seemed to defer to her judgment out of respect. Thus, Alice had almost no opportunity to observe appropriate methods of dealing with conflict, anger, frustration, or any other healthy expression of feeling. It was especially difficult for her to confront someone about things that were an infringement on her personal needs.

Alice's husband, Sam, on the other hand, grew up within a paternalistic tradition where the man of the family ruled and everyone was supposed to listen and obey. The men expressed their concerns and frustration very openly. In addition, they were very driven, aggressive risk-takers in their business practices. The women on his side of the family were subservient on most issues and thus avoided conflict. Like Alice, Sam had no experience learning how to resolve communication conflicts effectively and diplomatically. Rather, he displayed much of the same dominant behavior exhibited by his father, though it was considerably modulated by comparison.

Sam's father was known to be quite tyrannical and explosive in his family relationships. Sam was very reserved compared to his dad, but he couldn't resist the tendency to function by dominating in the relationship with Alice. This behavior served to fuel many arguments throughout life. He wanted something and she often resisted. Huge differences existed between them about effective communication, nurturing relationships, and coping with conflict. Neither was aware of the differences in values and beliefs that tormented them throughout their married life and ultimately led to their divorce.

Ironically, during the early years, while Alice and Sam had very few personal assets and were working hard to build their business, they got along fine. Perhaps it was because there was little time off from work and no major decisions that could become opportunity for conflict. However, after her mother moved to Florida for health reasons, Alice became more adamant in expressing her individual views on right and wrong.

Alice was very concerned about saving money and resources, minimizing risk, and the rightness of being extra-ordinarily nice to others while refraining from any negative emotions. By contrast, Sam was less tactful and somewhat callous in his communication with others. In addition, he was relatively unconcerned about saving resources; rather, he was willing to take many risks in order to get ahead in his plumbing business. Obviously, Alice and Sam had many opportunities for conflict.

Making **DO** out of **Doo-Doo**

The lesson in life from this lengthy introduction to family issues and alcohol use is the fact that Alice and Sam were on a collision course with regard to their values, beliefs, and innate behaviors. Nearly everything Sam did — personally and in business — was in direct opposition to Alice's values and beliefs. Similarly, Alice's conservatism and criticism aggravated Sam and he reacted loudly, causing hurt feelings and anger in Alice.

This is the background of how the alcohol became a problem for Alice in the beginning. Alice and Sam had serious personality differences, and Sam usually got his way in business affairs. Alice was bothered by his decisions and by the fact that she had no control. Alcohol became the substitute for better understanding and communication, ultimately contributing to alcoholism for Alice.

In spite of the alcohol issues, Alice's strength of character is truly phenomenal. She is identified as a wonderful person in her community, notwithstanding the problems that alcohol caused for her and her family over the years. Her ability to function and the significant contribution she has made to many people's lives is truly impressive.

The kids that Sam and Alice raised are well adjusted and seem to function very well in their professional lives. However, the alcohol issue and the depression issues probably exist as much with the kids as they did for Alice in her early adult years. Ironically, Alice's inability to take care of her own emotional needs caused many of the same problems among her kids. They learned by observation how to be compromising, especially in their ability to recognize feelings and communicate effectively. Relationship problems, questionable alcohol/drug abuse, gambling, and other addiction problems are common among families where communication problems exist.

I have had many clients like Alice's kids who grew up in alcoholic families that fit the title of adult children of alcoholic parents (ACOA). Many were unaware of or in denial for years about the impact of their childhood experiences in an alcoholic family. Sometimes habit patterns develop as a result of exposure to powerful family influences regarding conflict and control.

Commonly, there is a lack of role modeling and guidance regarding effective communication and appropriate methods for coping with stress. Relationship problems exist for everyone in the family, simply because of the upheaval that occurs with stifled communication and/or hostile and explosive verbal interactions. We should teach our children better ways to handle conflict or the effects of unresolved anger.

Lessons in Life

- If you abstain from alcohol usage — that's wonderful.
- If you choose to consume alcohol, keep in mind that over-indulgence to deal with intense emotions can cause many health problems and potential abuse issues.
- Communicating feelings in an open, non-hurtful, non-vindictive manner is absolutely essential in every family environment.
- Find a way to talk to a loved one about their drinking behavior if it causes you some concern.

Action Solutions

- Please reflect upon your personal use of alcohol or other mood-enhancing chemicals and make notations about changes you might like to make.

_____

_____

- Take note of others on your list of family and friends whom you may be concerned about in regard to alcohol use and abuse.

_____

_____

- Consider whether you need to confront someone whose behavior is self-destructive in this manner. How would you go about such a confrontation?

_____

_____

A Jar of Marshmallow Creme

As a young child, I witnessed my mother making fudge to deliver to family and neighbors as holiday gifts. After bugging her incessantly about scraping and licking the remainder of the "goodies" from the marshmallow creme jar, I was often saddened by how little there was left for me when my appetite for it was so big.

I pledged to someday buy my own jar of marshmallow creme and devour the entire jar by myself. It happened when I was a sophomore in college. I had worked in the police department long hours to cover my college expenses and had finally gotten enough disposable income that I could finally buy the jar of marshmallow creme just for me. After a delightful experience of consuming the entire jar in one sitting, I discovered how "pigging out" on something that sweet can come back to make you suffer the consequences of spontaneous over-consumption. I got sicker than I can ever remember and vomited so much that my insides were sore for a week. I learned a very important life-long lesson about the risks of over-indulgence.

I now try to eat very healthy and in moderation. The issues of disordered eating, obesity, anorexia, bulimia, body image, inactivity, continue to plague our citizens. I often wonder if we would have fewer problems if we just concentrated more on the quality and variety. Minimize the intake of high fat and high sugar foods and strive to be satisfied with a moderate quantity of food at each setting. Common sense and moderation should guide you in all your nutritional habits. You can be dealt a bum set of genes (high risk for heart disease, cancer, or some other chronic disease) and still live a long, healthy, and productive life.

When I ate that whole jar of marshmallow creme in one sitting, my body put on the brakes. In fact, my body rejected that stuff—the pain and agony of the puking was just not worth the delectable savoring of the sweet stuff going down. I think had I kept the food down, my body would have rejected it even further on the exit chute. Diarrhea was the only sick gastrointestinal symptom I did not experience that day.

Common sense might also suggest to us that having regular bowel eliminations is essential to health. Consuming plenty of fruits, vegetables, and water while being physically active could resolve most constipation problems. Beans are a great source of fiber. The effects may compromise your social life at times if you eat too much…however, they are great for your intestinal tract. Try to make a serious effort to consume more fruits and vegetables to increase your fiber intake. Exercise at least 20-30 minutes a day vigorously. Drink plenty of water (six-eight glasses a day) to help process all those fruits and veggies and to reduce your risk of colon cancer. I know this from personal experience, having watched my husband Red go through two life-threatening surgeries to extract cancerous tissue because he was too darn stubborn to eat properly and exercise as needed.

The next time you are selecting food or deciding whether to exercise, think about the fact that whatever you took in yesterday (by mouth) should be out the chute by today so it does not lie in the large bowel and contaminate your tissues. The cathartic effect of exercise is powerful as it stimulates regular bowel movements to ensure clean intestines and minimal rust-like stagnation.

Find some good information from reputable nutritionists or dieticians who have credentials to support their consultation. Remember, simple testimonials are not good reasons for you to buy a product or follow a plan. Be sure to use common sense and good judgment in selecting the source of your food products and nutritional plans, since profit-taking motives prevail among some advisors in this area.

Making **DO** out of **Doo-Doo**

Lessons in Life

- Eating excessively causes major problems, discomfort, and some health risk.

- Good nutritional philosophy is not based on counting calories but uses common sense, moderation, and variety.

- Fruits, vegetables, and beans (for fiber), regular exercise, and plentiful replenishment of fluids (drink lots of water) is important for healthy living and cleansing the G-I system on a daily basis.

Action Solutions

- Examine whether you have binged on food unnecessarily at some point in time.

_____

_____

_____

- Write down food choices for a day. How did you do with common senses, moderation, and variety?

_____

_____

_____

- Is there someone you know who should be concerned about food abuse or bad choice of foods?

_____

_____

_____

Spontaneous Consumption for Eating What Bugs You

Think back to a time when you might have wished you had known more of the facts before speaking out, or a time when you regret having said something in haste. Consider all those nagging "what ifs" and regrets. "Maybe if you'd have used a different tone," or "If you would have stopped and thought before having done or said something dumb." Maybe then the outcome might have been different. Learning how to own up to your mistakes instead of becoming defensive, angry, or explosive is a very important interpersonal skill. We never seem to know for sure whether it is better to express concerns openly or to suppress them in the presence of a family member.

Theresa's mother had bugged her daughter to go on a diet, to lose some weight. Her motives were very well-meaning. People told Theresa's mother that Theresa had such pretty features it was sad that she was a little overweight. Adults tend to meddle in each other's business without realizing the impact of their behavior. Physical appearance (fat or thin) became a regular topic of conversation and a major concern in Theresa's family. In addition, there were other conflicts going on that made the stress levels high for everyone, including Theresa. She was angry, but no one encouraged her to say what was bugging her. Food was always available and Theresa discovered that eating was a way of dealing with all the stress in the family. Food became a nurturing pacifier which served as a means of gratification to satisfy the gnawing pains of emotional upset. Stuffing her feelings by stuffing her stomach became a habit.

Theresa's mother was very concerned about the physical appearance of being overweight but failed to recognize the deeper feelings. Her conversations with Theresa focused upon diet, diet, diet without acknowledging the family conflicts or providing any other outlet. No one ever got close to the core issues of why Theresa was overweight. Talking about the body weight only exacerbated the overeating behavior.

Unfortunately, Theresa continued to gain weight well into her adult years reaching a weight of more than 300 pounds. The eating pattern had become such a habit that it became nearly impossible to change. Like Theresa, we all need to find better ways of using communication effectively and diplomatically to deal with emotions to avoid problems such as these. Sometimes it is better not to blow the symptoms out of proportion for kids in their developmental years where physical appearance is a factor. This is especially true when there are other underlying issues that have not yet been addressed.

Fortunately, Theresa has lost well over 100 pounds and is living a fairly healthy life, partly because she is very open about her feelings.

Hurt, anger, and embarrassment are very strong emotions. It is far better to acknowledge our mistakes and take ownership for human errors than to become defensive or attack others in an effort to correct a deeper problem. Wisdom is to know when to bite your tongue and not speak or when to confront the tougher issues instead of complaining about surface issues such as body weight. Keep your opinion to yourself or clean up the relationship issues that surround family concerns before you lapse into giving advice where it might not be appropriate.

Lessons in Life

- Parents, be aware that your patterns of eating and communicating will be copied by your kids. If you are not tuned in to healthy resolution of conflict, kids will act out the problem in some self-defeating way.

- Make the home environment a safe place to express feelings of anger or frustration. It is helpful to use conflicts as a way to teach diplomatic methods of communicating concerns.
- If you know someone who is gaining weight for no apparent reason, be cautious about what you say but consider the circumstances that might be influencing the behavior. Address the behavior rather than the eating.

Action Solutions

- Examine your own eating behaviors. Do you ever find that you eat beyond the point of hunger and that you eat to satisfy other needs such as loneliness, anger, upset, etc.?

_____

_____

_____

- Describe a situation where you might have observed a conflict situation that was not handled well and the people involved were stuck with bad feelings that were not resolved.

_____

_____

_____

- Plan how you might initiate a conflict resolution session with someone you care about who has difficulty expressing feelings especially in areas of conflict.

_____

_____

_____

Habits are Like a Soft Bed

Habits are like a soft bed; they're easy to get into but hard to get out of. But remember, you are trainable! When I was eight years old, I chewed my fingernails down to the very nubs. Biting at the last hangnail of each finger was painful and it was probably agonizing for my parents to watch the nervous habit as well. My mother wanted me to stop, but I couldn't. Week after week the nail-biting continued.

My mother must have had some great insight about behavior change, because she got me to stop chewing within a month, and I am pleased to say that I have never gone back to that nervous habit that plagued me for so long. My mother's strategy was to challenge me to a duel of comparable tasks. She asked me to identify one of her bad habits that I didn't like (I don't recall what it was and it really does not matter). What does matter is that she challenged me to show her that I could do better than she.

After the first couple of days, I was able to eke out a little growth on most of the nails because I was not chewing them. Right away she was extremely impressed. I can still hear those expressions of sincere amazement. She made a high pitched "gurgling" sound from her throat whenever she was surprised or impressed by something. I had heard that sound, throughout my childhood when other people impressed her. Thus I was especially pleased and delighted when I heard this sound and the words of encouragement from her indicating that I was winning the challenge.

Her reactions were due to both her satisfaction with my change and her frustration at not being able to change her own habit as fast as I was overcoming the nail-biting. I never knew whether my mom was seriously trying to beat me, but I know that hearing her expression of amazement was exactly what I needed at the time to break that difficult habit.

In each instance of working diligently to stop biting my nails, I can still hear the words and sounds of my mother encouraging me to know that I could do it and celebrate the results. I suppose we could conclude that I was pretty insecure at that age and that nail-biting held some deeper meaning. However, I know some very competent and successful adults who still chew their nails, so I am convinced that it is a very difficult habit to break.

I have managed to overcome a number of other such irritating habit patterns in my lifetime, although my wife thinks there are still plenty to work on. However, it is still the memory of my mother's encouragement and my personal success with breaking a childhood habit that gives me the confidence to address and change other such habits.

Lessons in Life

- All of us need a strong supporter to encourage us to take on a difficult challenge (like making or breaking a tough habit).
- Sometimes a challenge is just the motivation we need to step forward to healthier habits.
- By overcoming a small habit change (nail biting) we may grow to be able to take on more and more difficult challenges.
- Remember, it is never too late to develop new habits and if you ask for help, you may very well find someone to champion your way to success.

Making **DO** out of **Doo-Doo**

Action Solutions

• Describe a habit pattern that you would like to change.

_____

_____

_____

• What resources might help you change a habit or what advice do you need from others?

_____

_____

_____

• Describe what you need to do to make the necessary behavior changes.

_____

_____

_____

• What are the benefits and liabilities of this particular choice or solution?

_____

_____

_____

• What rewards and consequences can you use to reinforce success in this behavior change?

_____

_____

_____

Wake Up Sleepy Head, Get Up, Get Out of Bed

Every morning Dad would call from the bottom of the stairs to awaken me for chores and early fieldwork. Even though I really wanted to get up, I would usually fall back to sleep. Dad would return once or twice more, each time becoming a little more irritated. I just couldn't pry those eyelids open. In retrospect, I know that I must not have been getting enough restorative sleep. At that time, it didn't seem to matter when I got to bed at night, I would still sleep restlessly (bed sheets torn up and my hair all mussed), and I would never awaken feeling refreshed or eager to take on the day.

Even after college and well into my thirties, I had difficulty getting restful and restorative sleep. I never seemed to awaken rested and often was sleepy in the afternoons, especially if we were sitting around not actively engaged in stimulating movement. This pattern persisted until, one day, I read about the relationship between sleep apnea (restlessness) and snoring. Family members had told me, on occasion, that I snored and sometimes I stopped breathing while sleeping. I didn't believe them and ignored their advice until one afternoon I had fallen asleep on the couch and woke myself up with a rattling snort that startled me. Wow, was that ever embarrassing!

By reading the health literature, I discovered that the daytime sleepiness and poor quality sleep I had experienced for years were clearly related to sleep apnea and snoring. Sleep apnea means that I would snore for a while and then literally stop breathing for a period of 30-45 seconds. The breathless pe-

73

riod was then followed by a desperate gasp for air. This could happen 10-100 times a night and, obviously, disturb the quality of sleep.

With this information in hand, my doctor scheduled me for a sleep lab test (complete with all the brain wave wires and oxygen saturation measuring sensors). This test eventually revealed that I had a slight to moderate apnea condition. In addition to explaining my sleep problems, I discovered that the apnea condition, is also known to cause hypertension. I was relieved because, for most of my adult life, I had been plagued by a nagging problem with borderline hypertension. Salt restriction, exercise, diet, and stress reduction had not reduced my blood pressure, so I was hopeful that treating the apnea might take care of that problem, too. It did take care of the hypertension, and I am very grateful my family cared enough to suggest that I to look into the sleep disturbance problems (snoring and apnea).

While there are several medical treatments for apnea (including surgery), I found a different solution by way of my dentist. I happened to mention the recent sleep apnea discovery to him and was surprised to learn of an innovative dental appliance proven effective for apnea. My dentist devised a modified night-time bite plate (mouth guard) that extended my lower jaw forward, just a few centimeters, thus clearing my airway enough to stop most of the snoring and apnea. The result has been truly amazing. After forty years or more of apnea-induced sleep disturbance, I am now able to sleep with very little snoring or apnea and usually awaken refreshed, alert, and ready to go each morning. It has been such a dramatic relief that I have been amazed and somewhat irritated that I had to suffer for so many years before finding such a simple, easy, and inexpensive solution.

Lessons in Life

- If any of the following disturb your sleep, you may have a mild to moderate sleep disorder and should be tested in a certified sleep lab facility.
  - You snore often.
  - You are a restless sleeper.

- You are not alert and refreshed upon awakening in the morning.
  - You have day time sleepiness.
  - You fall asleep easily in a quiet situation.
- Other causes for potential sleep disturbance include muscle pain, joint discomfort, and strain. If you awaken frequently during the night and/or you find the bedding and your hair severely messed up upon awakening, you are probably a very restless sleeper.
- Eating a heavy meal or sweets/desserts together with caffeine in the late evening will effect the quality of your sleep. Excessive alcohol consumption may alter sleep patterns as well. While alcohol makes you sleepy initially, two to four hours later when the effects of the alcohol wear off, most people wake up or become restless.

Action Solutions

- Describe your sleep schedule and the quality of sleep that you get on average. _____

  _____

  _____

  _____

- What time do you awaken? _____
  - Do you use an alarm?_____
- Do you awaken in the middle of the night or early in the morning for no apparent reason? _____
- Are you usually refreshed upon arising in the morning?

  _____

- Do you have day-time drowsiness? _____
- List ways in which you could get more sleep and better quality sleep. _____

  _____

  _____

  _____

Hard Lessons for the Workaholic

People often make light of the fact that no one ever says, "I wish I'd spent more time at the office" in the autumn years of their life.

Betsy and Ralph came to see me for counseling. Actually, Betsy came in first for her headaches, and I came to the conclusion that her headaches might be related to her marital relationship. Her husband Ralph came in with her at my suggestion, but was clearly not very excited about my advice. Ralph had a full-time job plus he ran two other small businesses on the side. He was determined to be a very good provider for his family. Unfortunately, this meant that almost all the parenting responsibility was left to his wife, and he had very little time for her either. He was such a workaholic that he couldn't even take time for vacations. Betsy's brother gave her the use of a condominium for skiing in Colorado for a week over the holidays at no cost to the family. Ralph nixed the idea because he couldn't spare the time to get away.

In an effort to shake Ralph into some positive changes, I labeled the work we did as divorce counseling, i.e., figure out the financial consequences of not being able to work out your differences (a separation), then decide if it is worth your effort to make some changes. It was a paradoxical technique that worked very well. Ralph responded quite favorably, and the marriage survived, at least for a time. Betsy's headaches were somewhat improved and they stopped coming to counseling.

Unfortunately, the behavior change did not last. A couple of years later, I saw Betsy at a baseball game with the kids, but

Ralph was back to his old habits. Betsy seemed resigned to the situation. At least two more years went by. Then one day, I got a call from Ralph. He was very distressed. Betsy had served him with divorce papers. He acknowledged that he had lapsed back into his workaholic behavior and hardly knew his kids. Still, he became very angry mostly because the divorce settlement would obviously cut in half the college fund investments he had controlled for the kids. He did not trust that Betsy, his ex-wife-to-be, was capable of helping finance the needs of the kids in college, among other responsibilities.

It has now been seven years since that phone call in distress came in from Ralph. I have seen him regularly throughout that time period and have observed a remarkable transformation from his old self into a primary care-giver parent. Since the divorce, Ralph has developed a very close, loving, trusting relationship with both of his kids. He acknowledges unabashedly that the divorce was the best thing that could have happened in regard to his relationship with his kids. It forced him to wake up and pay attention to the needs of family and his own needs for a parenting role. *Making Do out of Doo-Doo* was very painful initially, but it serves as a constant reminder that one can gain more than they lose from a bad situation.

Betsy is doing well. She pursued an education, is gainfully employed, and works with Ralph about issues affecting the children.

Lessons in Life

- Keep your goals and aspirations in perspective. Family concerns are always more important than workaholic tendencies.

- Listen closely to those who care about you. Don't wait for the devastating "wake-up call" that may come too late, i.e., divorce or other family conflict.

- It is always possible to make the best of any situation and learn because of the hurts and disappointments.

- Setting an example for kids is very important.

Action Solutions

- What relationship issues cause you conflict?

_____

_____

_____

- List some of life's issues for which you need to apologize and make amends.

_____

_____

_____

- Describe a situation where you need to confront someone in a caring way about their behavior and its affect on others.

_____

_____

_____

Fire Power for Exercise

Attitude in action is the essential element in making any healthy change. Attitude is simply an idea fueled by emotion to make something good happen. Therefore since we know the critical information about the health benefits of exercise, and most people have the necessary skills and mobility to exercise regularly, why don't we just "get with it?" The missing ingredient is attitude. Sometimes the words of an outsider can provide the fire power for an attitude adjustment.

My firepower came from the hurtful but truthful remarks of my major advisor during my masters program at the University of Nebraska-Lincoln. During one of my final consultations before graduation, he startled me with two comments. The first was that I had great potential; the second was that I might not fulfill it because I was too fat. That was the firepower statement I needed to prove to him that I could become "Queen of Health and Physical Education" and lose weight. Now, more than twenty years have passed since I took the challenge from that harshly penetrating remark and made daily fitness a constant reminder that I must counter the obesity genes in my family. His challenge to be the best in my field is also fuel for my obsession to make us a healthier America.

During my teen and early adult years, I struggled with disordered eating, low self-concept, lethargy, and general unhappiness. However, by the time I got into my graduate work at the University of Nebraska-Lincoln, I had convinced myself that I could be a great teacher and a powerful health educator. The degree to which I was successful was duly noted by my advisor,

Dr. Landwer, who said to me, "JoAnne, you have the potential to be one of the leading females in our profession by the time you are forty." But my exhilaration about becoming "Queen of Health and Physical Education" was short-lived as he paused only a moment to add, "but you are too fat." His second comment about my weight took the wind out of my sails and jolted me into facing reality. He was right. I was overweight, very sedentary, and had poor nutritional habits. I became fat because I had not made physical activity a priority and I had eaten my way through the stresses of graduate school. Instead of becoming angry or defensive, I took his words as fuel for my fire.

Dr. Landwer's harsh words were a wake up call for me. I had used excuses to justify my unhealthy behaviors. I was stuck. Doc was right. Those harsh words were the nudge I needed to move me up the wellness ladder. Fourteen months after Doc gave me the "drop-kick" wake-up call, I had lost over forty pounds, dropped to fifteen percent body fat and won the first Lincoln Marathon in 3 hours, 23 minutes, 16 seconds.

One week after Doc confronted me with his truthful observation, I started my journey to a leaner, healthier body and ended up a marathoner. A brisk walk was the most I could get out of my body, but I really wanted to run. Telephone poles seemed like natural distance markers and thus the adventure began. I ran to a telephone pole, walked to the next, ran to the next, walked to another. After only about nine minutes of activity, the telephone pole turned from my natural incentive marker to the only thing I could find to hang on to as I would say, "Come on body, don't fail me now." My deep breathing (gasping for breath) routine could have passed for a Lamaze lesson. It was weeks before a mile did not seem like a trip across Nebraska. Telephone poles turned into miles and the miles added up. Marking accomplishments on a calendar was great reinforcement and satisfaction. My initial goal was to be able to run three miles without stopping. When that day came, it seemed logical to push just a little further and, wow…mark four miles on the calendar. Goals are powerful motivators and the day I marked six miles on the calendar I told Doc, "I can run a marathon." He said, "Yes you can!" I did and I won.

The activity seemed like the easier part of the weight loss challenge. The nutrition management was dreadful. I had adopted a philosophy, "Live to eat versus eat to live." Eating six miniature meals a day became a standard routine. Decreasing the food portions and increasing the quality of food choices allowed me to start changing my body size.

I still exercise daily and have just celebrated my twenty-third year in a peak performance body, yet I continue to strive for higher levels of wellness. Most people are uncomfortable making changes. The motivation or jump start we need may come as a harsh wake up call, but over the course of time proves to be the fire power we need.

Lessons in Life

- Knowledge, skills, and attitude are three necessary ingredients to achieve the health behavior you desire.

- Attitude can be influenced by motivation and the message may not always be in the form of "warm fuzzies." Try not to over-react to perceived criticism. Think about the message instead of the delivery. Heed the words in the message.

- Good physical skills are essential before pursuing any task. You must continue to use and improve the functioning of your body to the best of your ability. From the upper body strength needed to propel oneself in a wheelchair to working in the yard or garden, some activity is much better than being sedentary.

- Pay attention to the health indicators that reflect your need for change. For example, can you still fit in the clothes you wore ten years ago?

Disclaimer: You should consult a physician before beginning an exercise program if you (1) have been sedentary, (2) use tobacco products, (3) have a family history of heart disease, and/or (4) are recovering from serious illness.

Action Solutions

- Become a more informed consumer about health impacting issues such as nutrition, exercise, safety, finances, stress, relationships, faith, etc. Where can you obtain this information?

- Please take the time to list the benefits of exercise that are important for you: weight loss and/or maintenance, more energy, better sleep, etc.

  _____

  _____

  _____

  ▪ Other benefits _____

    _____

    _____

    _____

- Do you feel better when you are exercising regularly?

  _____

  _____

  _____

- Do you have less difficulty maintaining your weight?

  _____

  _____

  _____

In Closing...

While you are reading our message in these stories, you may be prompted to recall your own life experiences. Furthermore, you may be moved to take on a change for the better in some health-enhancing behavior.

We hope you have developed many lifetime physical activity skills such as swimming, bicycling, soccer, racquetball, walking, strength training, and many other sport skills as well as avocational pleasures including hiking, skiing, etc.

Attitude in many cases seems to be the "stickler," i.e., it may be very difficult to attain a good attitude about exercise if you have had unpleasant experiences with physical activity in the past.

It shouldn't be that difficult, however, to simply get motivated for some personal reason (I want to be happier and more healthy) and to make the necessary attitude adjustment about taking charge and just doing it. Some of the aspects of motivation are known but in most cases, the individual just has to examine his/her conscience to answer the question, "Why should I do this?" and "What will I gain by doing it?" As a starting point, list the factors that motivate you to take on a task.

Sometimes the best way to get started with anything is to be safe and cautious, but charge ahead. Ready, fire, aim!

Part II

It Is Hard to Create a Great Thing Suddenly

In our society, there seems to be an obsession with instant gratification. Whether it is the designer jeans that our children want us to buy for them or the ten pounds we want to lose, right now (or yesterday) is generally the preferred time frame for getting what we want. Developing a sense of delayed gratification also applies to other health behaviors. You have probably heard that "anything worth having is worth waiting for." Developing and maintaining health-enhancing behaviors is a lifelong endeavor and "well" worth your time, investment, and energy. Your life-long health enhancement routines should include: aerobic exercise, strength & flexibility activity, nourishment, hydration, rest and sleep, stress management, positive thinking, humor, strong social support, and belief in a higher power (e.g., spiritual faith).

Make the time investment, practice the healthy concepts, be patient, and then you can expect the rewards of your health, hardiness, and fitness efforts. Having high level wellness and a peak performance body should be a lifelong goal. Investing in oneself is something most people have to develop over time. Be patient and make your life-long health goals into habits. Recognize that it takes time, a long time, to achieve and maintain a pattern of health enhancing behaviors. It is hard to create a great thing suddenly.

Go For the Goal

Does the word procrastination ring a bell? The important question is "If it's good for us, why don't we just do it?" Whether the task is beginning and maintaining an exercise program, doing taxes, or cleaning out the closet and garage, we sometimes just can't seem to "get a move on." Could it be the stakes are not high enough or the consequences not severe enough to motivate us to action? Heart attack patients seem to have no difficulty becoming motivated to make health behavior changes in diet, exercise, etc. Do you have to wait for some health disaster so you then have to *Make Do out of Doo-Doo*?

You can be in control of living longer and better with the decision to "Get off it." Get off the couch and get into action. "Get off your duff and strut your stuff" is a common statement we make to our audiences. Making a lifetime commitment to daily health enhancing choices can add "life to your years and years to your life." Why wait until the first of the month, the New Year, your birthday, or a heart attack to get started in a program? If you are not ready to make a commitment today, then you have already made a decision about priorities. The *lessons in life* are *do your best, be your best,* and *enjoy the rewards of health, hardiness, and fitness.*

The Secret of Success Is To Begin

- Setting reasonable goals is the first step in developing a health enhancing, high performance lifestyle. Make sure your goals are meaningful and challenge you to become better. Losing weight and being more active are meaningful goals for over half of all Americans. The tough question is "How do you make your goals come true?"

- It is important to have passion for the goals you wish to achieve in life. How do you become impassioned? Sometimes a dramatic event results in an emotional life change. The teenager, saved by the surgeon who removed her brain tumor, was motivated to attend medical school and eventually served others in the same way her life was saved. That is one way of becoming motivated, but we shouldn't have to experience a traumatic event in order to become impassioned about our lifestyle issues. What is the driving force that will make you successful in reaching your goals?

- People who are successful at reaching their goals usually have a strong role model. How do you discover the important role models in your life? Typical role models include parents, older siblings, uncles, aunts, grandparents, teachers, and friends who exhibit some image we admire or behavior we want to achieve. Be sure that you choose role models whose image and/or behaviors are healthy.

- Explore the health enhancing activities that your role model exhibits. Ask questions to find out what he/she did to become successful in achieving and maintaining that behavior.

- Learn about your family's medical history. What Mom, Dad, Grandma, and/or Grandpa struggled with many years ago may help you anticipate your future health risks. Find out your strengths and weaknesses; what are your genetic vulnerabilities? If diabetes, cancer, heart disease, and/or gastrointestinal disorders are part of your family history, you may be wise to take special precautions in diet, stress reduction, exercise and medical screening practices.

- Learn from all your behavior change experiences, especially the negative ones. Past failures in New Year's resolutions to exercise or diet merely illustrate what does not work for you. When disappointments occur in life, remember to *Make Do out of Doo-Doo*. Bounce back from every difficult situation and try to grow, thus benefitting from the "natural fertilizer of life." Remember, *Doo-Doo Happens*. Find some program of behavior change you can tolerate to achieve your health enhancement goals. How about starting with exercise right now?

Health Benefits of Regular Exercise

- Physically active individuals reduce their risk of developing coronary heart disease by a factor of two.
- Exercise improves health-risk profiles by lowering blood pressure, reducing body fat, improving lipid profiles, and reducing risk of adult-onset diabetes.
- Exercise delays the aging process and maintains good muscle tone.
- Stretching exercises increase flexibility and improve posture.
- Exercise promotes muscular relaxation and helps relieve muscle tension and fatigue.
- Exercise improves appetite and digestion, and facilitates sleep onset and quality.
- Exercise, in moderation, improves immune function and may prevent some common contagious illnesses such as colds and flu.
- Exercise increases energy, endurance, and clarity of thinking.
- Exercise builds self-concept and positive attitude, and reinforces commitment to make other personal changes.
- Exercise clearly improves psychological, as well as physical, well-being by relieving stress, anxiety, and depression.

Top Ten Excuses Why People Choose "NOT" to Exercise

We tend to ignore, avoid, or put off tasks we do not like, but know must be done. Many of the reasons we give to justify our procrastination are based on bad judgment. Good people often make bad choices in life. Consider these examples:

10. *I hate to exercise almost as much as I dislike housework.* Therefore, I have some options: (a) live in dirt and disorganization (not a pleasant thought), (b) just do it and pretend that I am having a great time; or (c) hire it done. Unfortunately, exercise for hire is not an option. You must do it yourself, so-o-o-o-o get off your duff and pretend you are having a good time. You may actually enjoy it.

9. *I have an injury.* Use whatever body parts are still functioning and continue to be moderately active to keep the joints or muscles functioning while healing (under supervision of a trainer or rehabilitation specialist, if necessary). For example, swimming is very good exercise when you have shin splints, an ankle sprain, or a knee injury because it minimizes the strain and pressure induced by gravity-based exercise such as jogging.

8. *It's hard work.* This is not an acceptable excuse. By comparison, housework is hard work. Not only that, but doing dishes, cleaning up messes, and scrubbing toilets can be hazardous to your health. You just have to get off this

hang-up about the effort involved in exercise and know that the hard work is worth it. Another suggestion is to find someone to exercise with you and talk. You won't notice the physical effort it takes.

7. *I hate my own body.* This is commonly described as "stinkin' thinkin'," or negative self-talk. Most people have some body feature that they feel is unacceptable (shape of nose, hair texture, lack of hair, too much of this, too little of that). Rather, you need to appreciate what you do have. Exercise, sleep, nutrition, hydration, and hygiene are essential for "your body to feel good and for you to feel good about your body." If you let it become rusty and dysfunctional from disuse, where are you going to live?

6. *If I need to feel good, I'll smoke it, drink it, or pop a pill.* NOT A GOOD SOLUTION! It would be best if you eliminate this temptation. The over-use of substances including food, alcohol, tobacco, and over-the-counter medicines may provide some satisfaction and temporary relief of fatigue, minor aches or pain, and emotional distress. However, regular dependence on these can cause more serious physical and mental complications.

5. *I have too many work and family commitments.* Of course you may think that you don't have time to exercise because of the needs of your job and family. However, this is even more reason to get off your excuses and take care of yourself so you can handle the workload. How can you be a fully responsible person if your health has deteriorated or you die prematurely of a heart attack? So take care of yourself, for the sake of your family. They will appreciate it greatly.

4. *It is too hot, too cold, too wet outside, etc.* Find an indoor facility for exercise or consider bad weather a challenge to overcome that will make you tougher in the future. You could get up earlier (if it is hot outside), dress more heat efficiently (if it is cold outside), or you could be creative in finding alternate exercise (climb stairs in a hotel, if it is raining). Use common sense and prudence about exercising outdoors during the hottest or coldest times of the day and think of your exercise as an adventure.

3. ***I'm too tired.*** You are more than likely mentally fatigued, not physically tired. Your other lifestyle habits (sleep, hydration, diet, time management, etc.) might explain the mental fatigue. Once you overcome the initial resistance to exercise, you may become invigorated. Be sure to pick an activity that you enjoy. Once you "get in shape," you will eventually have more energy. If you have persistent fatigue or you are a woman dealing with menopausal changes including fatigue and sleep disruption, you should see a physician.

2. ***I don't have enough time in my schedule.*** Maybe you need better time management or a change in your job, perhaps learning to delegate more to others. It only takes 30 minutes a day, four to five times a week of walking, cycling, jogging, or swimming to achieve the desired health benefits. Even yard work, housework, raking leaves, and shoveling snow can help burn calories while accomplishing some necessary work. You might find that you can include exercise as a part of a commute to and from work. Walking from the train to your car or home, parking at the far end of the parking lot, or bicycling to work can make you feel good about saving both time and money while getting where you need to go.

1. ***And... the Number One bad excuse not to exercise is that you are just lazy and exercise is simply not a high priority in your life.*** You must take charge of this issue and set a schedule. For some people, mornings are best, because then it's done and you can get on with the day. Be smart, safe, and do it!

Other chapters in Part I of the book may help with your attitude and motivation. You might want to reread the chapter entitled "Firepower for Exercise" to help you get over the obstacles listed and then get on with what needs to be done for the "health of it."*

*If you need information about quality physical education programming in your school system, contact the National Association for Sport and Physical Education (800-213-7193 ext. 461).

Getting Beyond the Excuses and Into a Program

So what can we do to help you find the appropriate method of exercise that fits your routine and your enjoyment needs. Please consider the following questions designed to help you discover your exercise/activity/fitness options specifically for health enhancement.

- Have you ever been in very good physical condition? When was that and how old were you?

_____

  - What were the circumstances when you were in good physical condition, i.e., was it part of your work, leisure or sport conditioning?

  _____

- Do you recall advantages to being in good physical condition? What were they for you, e.g., feel good, lower weight, etc.?

_____

- What recreational activities do you enjoy, e.g., walking, hiking, biking, swimming, gardening, racquetball, basketball, tennis, etc.?

_____

- What opportunities do you have to engage in your chosen activity? Do you have access to YMCA/treadmill/swimming pool/tennis?

  - What exercise resources could you access with little or no additional cost to you?

- Do you prefer exercising with someone for companionship or do you prefer to exercise alone?

  - If you prefer companionship, who could be your partner?

- What has prevented you from continuing a regular exercise program in the past, e.g., bad weather, lack of time, minor injury, etc.?

  - What do you need to do to prevent that problem in the future?

- Do you have any strong motivations for maintaining an exercise program, e.g., losing weight, lowering blood pressure, controlling diabetes, enhancing mood and feeling of well-being, etc.?

  - How can you be motivated to follow through on your exercise program?

- What is your ideal program of exercise, e.g., biking, basketball, swimming or volksmarch? Describe the enjoyment, challenge, and rewards that result from these activities.

_____

- When do you plan to start and how are you going to maintain a regular pattern of activity, e.g., starting tomorrow you might walk three times a week and go for a hike in the country on the weekend.

_____

- If your time problems are overwhelming, consider the following non-traditional exercise options to save time and get functional things done while you exercise.

    - *Commute to work. Ride a bike in good weather, walk to and from a train or distant parking lot.*

    - *Hike or bike with a child. Invest in back pack/front pack or childproof baby/bike seat to eliminate childcare concerns during exercise.*

    - *Use the fire escape stairs.* To get to and from your room in a hotel going up and down the stairs repeatedly can be a great workout.

    - *Get some exercise equipment*: a rowing machine, a stair stepper and/or aerodyne stationary bicycle. Use these while watching television.

    - *Exercise early in the day.* This will inspire and invigorate you to complete the rest of the day's activities.

    - *Do housework to the music of your choice.*

    - *Exercise with a television aerobics program.*

    - *Dance to your favorite music at home or out with friends.*

You Are What You "Chews" (choose) to Eat

Eating is one activity most of us take for granted. Many factors influence when, what, and how much we eat. Social pressures, sensory stimulation, family traditions, emotional distress, and celebrations can all entice us to eat. Economic factors may determine the type and quality of food we purchase, but cultural factors influence how it is prepared (e.g., fried or broiled). Changing the way you think about food can enable you to eat to live rather than live to eat.

Today we have dietary choices, information, and nutritional challenges our grandparents never had to face. Simply put, to reduce your risk of heart disease, cancer, and other chronic diseases, you must consider the following dietary guidelines about the "food you chews."

- Don't eat more than you can burn off through activity/exercise.
- Cut down on fats (animal and vegetable).
- Cut down on cholesterol (found only in foods of animal origin).
- Cut down on salts and sugars.
- Broil, bake, or barbeque rather than frying.
- Follow Grandma's advice and eat your oatmeal, fruits, and vegetables.

Making **DO** out of **Doo-Doo**

Think about your body and food choices as a savings and loan. If we deposit more calories into our bodies than we burn off on a daily basis, a savings account is set up — called *fat*. If the daily calorie deposit is used up, no fat savings plan will be started. If we limit the daily caloric deposits, the fat account could be overdrawn and we'll lose weight. As you determine if you want to lose, gain, or maintain your savings and loan plan (e.g., weight and energy level), the following tips should be helpful.

- Think in terms of a nutritional plan rather than a diet. If you underline the first three letters in the word diet — you will have "die." Work at understanding the relationship between your body's physiological needs and the ingredients in food that help you accomplish daily routines.

- Know your nutrients. Proteins, carbohydrates, fats, vitamins, minerals, and water are all essential for high level wellness. Use common sense to achieve balanced daily eating habits and start the day with a good breakfast.

- Know what you are putting in your mouth. Read and understand labels and work at being a wise consumer.

- "Chews," or *choose*, lean meats, poultry, and fish. Remove skin and fat and broil or bake whenever possible.

- When you eat, don't do anything but eat. Enjoy your food and be aware of how much you are eating.

- Grocery shop with a carefully planned list. This will help you avoid impulse purchases.*

- Fruit, fresh vegetables, and whole-grains will fill you up — not out.

- Alcoholic drinks have a significant number of calories.

- Learn to distinguish stomach hunger (stomach growl) from mouth hunger (wanting something to chew on).

- Limit your caffeine intake. Caffeine is an appetite stimulant that may thwart your efforts if you are trying to lose weight.

*If you need help planning nutritious meals, losing weight, making wise consumer decisions, or finding good nutrition information, consider contacting a "Counseling Nutritionist." Look for a counseling nutritionist who has a RD (Registered Dietitian) credential.

- Keep busy. People who are busy rarely have time to think about food.
- Eat regularly. Skipping meals can make you think you deserve to eat more when you do eat.
- Manage your weight and food choices because you *are* a wonderful person—not in order to become one.

If You Need an Alarm—You Are Short on Sleep

Scientists are finding that cutting back on the number of hours we sleep may be as dangerous as poor diet and physical inactivity. On average, we need about eight hours of sleep per night (some of us need more or less, ranging from six to ten hours per night). If you need an alarm clock to awaken in the morning, you have not gotten enough sleep. Unfortunately, most of us get much less sleep than we need (by at least one hour per night) as reflected by the level of daytime sleepiness that interferes with our daily activities.

When we don't get enough sleep, stress levels are increased dramatically. A very potent stress hormone, cortisol, is released in higher quantities when we are short on sleep. If sleep deprivation continues for several days, we can develop immune function deficiency resulting in an increase in colds, flu, and infections together with some memory impairment and premature aging. Other sleep deprivation effects include increased irritability, depression, paranoia, energy loss, hormone deficiency, and possible brain cell damage.

Sleep Deprivation and Accidents

If you tend to fall asleep easily and somewhat inappropriately, i.e., sitting in a quiet movie or concert, it means that you are short on sleep. The sleep/wake center in the brain takes over in a restful circumstance when you are over-tired and dumps you into a sleep state, even if you would prefer to stay awake and be productive. Driving can be monotonous and make you drowsy. Just sitting in a relaxed position while driving may make you sleepy and increase your risk for an accident. One out of every four drivers has fallen asleep at the wheel (due to momentary lapses called micro-sleep) and about 100,000 car crashes each year are blamed on sleepy drivers.

Struggling to stay awake causes most people to become fidgety and restless because of the increased tension produced in the body's natural effort to fight off drowsiness and stay alert. Some people are inclined to consume coffee and caffeine-based drinks to stay awake. While caffeine provides some temporary wakefulness, it may compound the problem. Even one cup of coffee consumed early in the day causes a measurable amount of restless sleep that evening. Those who consume a great deal of caffeine throughout the day are likely to have more severe sleep disruption symptoms. You may not be aware of the caffeine-related symptoms during sleep, but the difficulty awaking in the morning and the daytime sleepiness are the ultimate measures of sleep disturbance and your sleep deprivation needs.

If you know that you are short on sleep during busy periods of work but you must remain alert and attentive, consider various ways of staying actively involved. Sometimes it helps to stand and move around while reviewing important papers that require careful deliberation. During some informal meetings or conferences where alertness, creativity, and strategic decision-making skills are needed, it may be very appropriate to stretch or even walk around during the discussions. The change of pace may be a helpful stimulant for others as well.

If you become sleepy while driving, you are in a serious high-risk situation. Consider rolling the window down on a cool day, chew on a slice of lemon, listen to upbeat music, or do some resistance exercise against the floor board or the steering wheel. A safer and healthier option is to stop for a short while in a safe area and take a quick nap. Twenty minutes of daytime sleep could rejuvenate your mental batteries and prevent a serious accident.

Tips for Better Quality and Quantity of Sleep

- Pay attention to your sleep/wake cycle and the indications of sleep deprivation. *Yawning often throughout the day and drowsiness while reading or driving are indications that you need more sleep.*

- If an alarm clock starts your day because you absolutely need it to awaken, you are short on sleep. You should be able to wake up at an appropriate start time in the morning automatically.

- If your wake up experience (by alarm or wake-up call) is startling or very disturbing to you, then you probably didn't get to sleep early enough the night before.

- If you feel overwhelmed with daytime sleepiness, either get some physical activity (walk around, go outside while conversing) or take a nap.

- Try to go to bed and get up on a regular schedule. Getting up in the morning at a consistent time strengthens the circadian cycle and helps with evening sleep onset.

- Keep the bed for the purpose of sleep and sex only. Watching television, eating, drinking, or playing games in bed tends to create confusion for your mind and body. The bedroom environment should have many sleep cues (comfortable pillow, soothing pictures, etc.) that lead toward sleep onset.

- Avoid caffeine four to six hours before bedtime. Remember, most soft drinks, tea, and chocolate all have caffeine which can disturb sleep even if you don't feel it immediately. Avoid heavy meals in the last few hours before bedtime.

- Be aware that alcohol and other sedative substances may help induce sleep but, like caffeine, they can disturb sleep a few hours after sleep onset. Alcohol-induced sleep onset is very quick, but the quality of sleep is fragmented and you never reach the deep restorative level that is needed.

- Chronic use of tobacco products may disturb sleep or prevent sleep onset. The stimulant effects are counterproductive to sleep.

- If you have difficulty getting to sleep because of some emotional issue (frustration, anger, excitement, etc.), perhaps it is better to get up and do something about the issue such as writing about it or completing a boring task which makes you sleepy just thinking about it.

- Whenever possible, allow yourself to awaken without an alarm clock. The startle effects of the alarm are moderately traumatic, causing some stress reactions.

- Obviously there are times when you will be short on sleep for various reasons. Allow some opportunities for a daytime nap or to crash early in the evening to catch up appropriately. If you have worked hard during the sleep deprivation time, then you deserve the extra rest upon completion of the task.

- If you suspect that you have apnea or a sleep disorder (based on information provided in Part I), have someone monitor your sleep periodically. Have a tape recording of your breathing while sleeping. Request that your physician consider prescribing a sleep lab test.

Tips for Effective Stress Coping

In Part I of this book, we shared numerous stories of lessons in hardiness, health, and fitness we have learned. Though many of these scenarios were very stressful at the time, the eventual outcomes proved to be great long-term learning experiences. It is important to learn about new methods of stress coping while also identifying indicators of stress and tension experiences.

Regardless of what might provoke a stress reaction, we can be aware of the wide variation in signs and symptoms of stress. Some of these (like nervous fidgeting or cold, sweaty hands) are clear and undeniable, while others (like nervous stomach and anxiety) are subtle but critically important. Just noticing these manifestations among the others such as trembling hands, fidgeting, perspiration (on forehead or underarms), nervous laughter, and irritability is enough to alert some people that they are under too much stress.

Take notice next time you are in a social gathering where you are obliged to shake hands with several people consecutively. Upon careful observation, you may note that some have either cold or sweaty hands, or both. They may or may not be noticeably excited or distressed, but the cold and/or sweaty hands reveal their true state of emotion at that moment. Consider also the inexperienced speaker who is faced with a large audience and a difficult presentation. Recall that there is always a pitcher of water near the podium because one of the classic stress symptoms is "cotton mouth." This occurs because the salivary glands in the mouth shut down and/or produce very sticky material under stress.

Many people are totally unaware of their personal profile of stress signs and symptoms. With some insight, we should be able to link these symptoms to the apparent apprehension, fear, or anger. To control stress, you must first acknowledge the symptoms. Only then, can you adapt or take precautions to avoid similar situations.

There are many medical disorders known to be associated with failure to deal with high levels of stress. These include such physical manifestations as: headache, hives, alopecia (sudden, unexpected hair loss), hypertension, irritable bowel, and hyper-hydrosis (sweaty hands), as well as several psychological issues such as anxiety, panic, phobia, depression, and severe anger.* In the absence of serious medical stress-related disorders, and with the benefit of good judgment and a little skill development, we can usually benefit from some general knowledge and basic recommendations regarding stress.

Consider the following tips for dealing with unavoidable stress:

- Learn to recognize your personal profile of early warning signs of stress (e.g., nervous stomach, neck and back tightness or discomfort, fatigue, irritability, unnecessary worry, cold/sweaty hands, etc.).

- Identify what is going on in your life that might be stressful, and then make a rational appraisal of how realistic this circumstance is in terms of threat, risk, potential happiness, sadness, etc.

- Consider if the stressful situation seems to be related to your signs of stress (Do the stress symptoms come and go along with the stressful circumstances?). Then decide if the situation is worth all the distress it is apparently causing for you.

- If the stress situation is definitely worth the distress, then take vigorous immediate action to resolve or overcome the situa-

*For any of these disorders, seek assistance from a qualified biofeedback therapist or health care professional who specializes in treating stress-related disorders. Biofeedback therapy, counseling, and relaxation skills are excellent non-pharmaceutical treatments you might consider.

tion (study for test, look for job) and consider being creative or assertive to resolve it.

- Determine if the situation is really worth getting upset over by applying a "reality test." (Is the stressor life threatening or just somewhat embarrassing?) Most stressors are inconsequential and diminish over time.

- If you still can't stop thinking about a stressful event even though it is not worth getting upset over, do some "thought stopping" (wear a rubber band on your wrist that you snap hard to stop a repeating thought).

- Go for a walk or exercise vigorously to temporarily modulate your stress reactions and allow some time to cool off and think rationally.

This short list of stress coping techniques is intended to help you minimize your immediate distress and help you downgrade an acute stressor to a minor hassle. This minor hassle can be put aside for the moment, allowing you to deliberate more seriously over a resolution. In the long run, there are better techniques to protect yourself with lifestyle health-enhancing stress coping.

Other stress coping strategies include:

- Take better care of yourself: get proper nutrition, enough sleep, exercise, hydration, leisure, and recreation; minimize alcohol, caffeine, and eliminate other unnecessary substance use.

- Develop a positive outlook on the future: decide what you need to change and then let go of unnecessary worries and concerns; become an optimist.

- Be kind to others and look for others to do the same: respect the feelings of others and expect it in return; be diplomatically assertive about your needs and concerns.

- Take a little deeper breath than usual, filling your abdomen and blowing out to let go of any tension in your shoulders, neck, and back every time you exhale.

- Manage your time well and allow opportunities to relax your face, neck, arms, hips, and legs; minimize undue effort in these areas when driving, typing, reading, etc.

- Change sitting position and type of desk activity every few minutes to prevent strain and overuse disorders in typing or other repetitive tasks.

- Learn to be functionally relaxed: you may need to take a course in progressive relaxation, meditation, or biofeedback to gain these skills.

- Be assertive about your needs without being aggressive or vindictive; using diplomacy, you can usually let others know your boundaries while enhancing their respect and appreciation of you.

- Develop a strong self-image: strive to achieve what you desire and be proud of what you have; a high level of self-concept may insulate you from many of the disappointments and frustrations of life.

Temporary Loss Can be a Long Term Gain in Making Do out of Doo-Doo

There is an old saying: "We gain the most after we lose something we value." After many losses and gains over a lifetime, these words take on significant meaning and remind us of lots of lessons in life. Are you going to wait until you have a major loss or health crisis before you take action on your health behavior changes? When you put down this book, we challenge you to walk away from your health-debilitating behaviors and "walk the talk" of health enhancing behaviors.

Please consider the following questions and post them on your bathroom mirror. The purpose will be two-fold. You will have an excuse for having a bad hair day (can't see through the notes) and they will be your daily reminder about how to *Make Do out of Doo-Doo* while taking charge of your hardiness, health, and fitness.

- Why is it most people get more serious about health enhancing choices after age 45 or 50 when their health begins to diminish?

- Why do some families only get together at the time of the death of a loved one?

- Why do we wish we had said and done more for a person only after they have died?

- Why do some people get more serious and devoted to faith and prayer during or after a traumatic incident?

- Why do we get more serious about home safety only after someone in "our neighborhood" has been victimized?

By now, you should understand the concept of temporary loss being a potential gain. Perhaps you could even add to the list of questions above. However, the most useful lesson to be gained from losing anything in life is how to spend our lives being more centered. Being centered means that, at the end of every day, we have a sense of contentment, a sigh of relief, and a big smile that says, "If I die in my sleep tonight, my checklist is complete. No more days of 'woulda, shoulda, coulda'." You could have more days of, "I did it."

Yes, I ...

- am making fewer health debilitating choices and more health enhancing choices today.

- am making a commitment to get to the next family reunion (or "rebellion") and perhaps I will organize it myself.

- am trying every day to know more about faith and the power of prayer in my life.

- will take the time to write the note, answer the e-mail, make the phone call, send the card/gift to make my positive feelings known to others I care about.

- will do an inventory about my home safety from lights to door locks and fire alarms to ventilation, etc.

- will develop and maintain new skills for hardiness, health, and fitness every day.

- will get to bed earlier and get up refreshed and eager to take on new challenges every day.

- will eat more nutritionally while staying physically active and managing my stress.

- will remind myself what a healthy person I am becoming. I am doing things right and doing the right things. I can look in the mirror and say "You sexy thing, don't you ever die! There is too *much work and fun* to be done!"

- will give thanks for the blessings in life and look for the positive in every life experience no matter how bad it appears to be. I can *Make Do out of Doo-Doo*.

This list goes on and so does your quest for health, happiness, hardiness, fitness, and a good life. Keep us posted on your struggles and success and feel free to "holler if you need something!"

About the Authors

Dr. JoAnne Owens-Nauslar is Director of Professional Development for the American School Health Association in Kent, Ohio. She lives on a ranch near Lincoln, Nebraska, where she and husband Red raise Texas longhorn cattle and quarter horses. JoAnne considers herself a Wyoming woman and therein lies her hardiness.

Dr. Jo is a health and physical educator who walks the talk while teaching lessons in life. As a Healthy American Fitness Leader, National Health Educator of the Year and Past President of the National Association for Sports and Physical Education, she speaks to thousands of young people and adults each year about *Making Do out of Doo-Doo*. Her dynamic, high-energy presentation style, health and performance message, combined with her wit and humor, allow her to present to members of the corporate world, teachers, youth, families, school administrators, school board members, and farmers/ranchers. Dr. Jo has experienced life's disappointments and always bounces back.

In addition to a doctorate in Education Administration, her most revered credential is L.B.W.A. (Learning By Wandering Around). Her constant message is to consider ways to enhance and strengthen your spirit for living and sense of hardiness through health and fitness.

Dr. Wes Sime is professor of Health and Human Performance at the University of Nebraska-Lincoln. A native of southern Minnesota he grew up on a farm and that remains a strong part of his heritage. Much of the hardiness and ingenuity he demonstrates as a professional is a result of the lessons he learned on the farm.

Dr. Sime has a PhD in both stress physiology and health psychology. He is a consultant to numerous individuals in farm/ranch industry, business and professional settings. He is also a dynamic speaker, sharing a message of stress hardiness and peak performance to groups all over the country and abroad. His research on effects of physical activity, mental/physical health, and well being has been presented in numerous national publications.

Dr. Sime is a personal counselor for many individuals seeking resolutions to major crises as well as routine hassles associated with adjustment when things just don't turn out well. Thus, the process of *Making Do out of Doo-Doo* fits the theme of the book very well. Dr. Sime has had numerous accidents, injuries and disappointments throughout his career, making him a role model to many who are trying to bounce back from the traumas and tragedies of living in a very hectic, stress-packed world.